Approaching the
ALMIGHTY

---

100 PRAYERS OF
A.W. Tozer

Approaching the
ALMIGHTY

100 PRAYERS OF
A.W. Tozer

Compiled by Philip Shappard

MOODY PUBLISHERS

CHICAGO

These prayers of A. W. Tozer were transcribed and edited from recorded sermons preached at Southside Alliance Church in Chicago, 1953–1959. Some dates and references have been omitted.

Edited by Kevin Mungons
Interior design: Puckett Smartt
Cover design: Charles Brock
Cover image of wave pattern copyright © 2020 by marukopum / Deposit Photos (418883948). All rights reserved.

Library of Congress Cataloging-in-Publication Data

Names: Tozer, A. W. (Aiden Wilson), 1897-1963, author. | Shappard, Philip, compiler.
Title: Approaching the Almighty : 100 prayers of A.W. Tozer / compiled by Philip Shappard.
Other titles: Prayers. Selections
Description: Chicago : Moody Publishers, [2021] | "These prayers of A. W. Tozer were transcribed from recorded sermons preached at Southside Alliance Church in Chicago, 1953-1959." | Includes bibliographical references. | Summary: "For the first time, Approaching the Almighty publishes the prayers that Tozer offered as he stepped into the pulpit to preach. Here are nearly two hundred prayers that reveal the great preacher's intimate walk with God. Let Tozer's pulpit prayers guide your own heart in its steadfast pursuit of God"-- Provided by publisher.
Identifiers: LCCN 2021022846 | ISBN 9780802424419 (hardcover) | ISBN 9780802499998 (ebook)
Subjects: LCSH: Prayers. | Christian life. | BISAC: RELIGION / Christian Living / Prayer | RELIGION / Prayerbooks / Christian
Classification: LCC BV245 .T69 2021 | DDC 242/.8--dc23
LC record available at https://lccn.loc.gov/2021022846

Originally delivered by fleets of horse-drawn wagons, the affordable paperbacks from D. L. Moody's publishing house resourced the church and served everyday people. Now, after more than 125 years of publishing and ministry, Moody Publishers' mission remains the same—even if our delivery systems have changed a bit. For more information on other books (and resources) created from a biblical perspective, go to www.moodypublishers.com or write to:

Moody Publishers
820 N. LaSalle Boulevard
Chicago, IL 60610

1 3 5 7 9 10 8 6 4 2

Printed in the United States of America

TABLE OF CONTENTS

INTRODUCTION

by Philip R. Shappard

MANY TRIBUTES HAVE BEEN WRITTEN and said of Aiden Wilson Tozer. His expressed thoughts on God have deeply impacted several generations of those who call upon Jesus Christ as Lord. Some may point to books such as *The Knowledge of the Holy* or *The Pursuit of God* as evidence of Tozer's keen insight to illuminate a seeking pilgrim's personal journey into the heart of God.

Possibly the greatest single impact of this self-educated man actually started on the floor of his Chicago church study as he would daily don his old prayer trousers and then, for a period of time, lay prostrate on the floor as he sought God.

"Everything that God has ever used in me to help others, He has given me on my knees with my open Bible," he said in a 1950s sermon. "God has been pleased to use the book *The Pursuit of God* far beyond the borders of the Christian and Missionary Alliance." He went on to describe his writing process: "In almost every chapter, I got on my knees with God alone seeking cleansing and power and purity and righteousness in my own spirit. Then, with a notebook, taking down notes, and from that, writing. Brethren, that's what we need, more than we need anything else in the wide world."

I first heard the recorded messages of A. W. Tozer when I was cueing them for broadcast on Moody Radio. I listened to them countless times during my forty-year career, but for some reason I failed to pick up on a distinctly different voice when this devoted man of God started praying. One day his prayer at the end of a message jumped out and captured my attention. In that moment, rather than hearing A. W. Tozer talk to his flock about God, I heard his voice become soft and reverent as he talked to God on behalf of those gathered before him.

As I transcribed and compiled these prayers from the original sermon recordings, I was careful to preserve his words with great fidelity. In other words, what you read is actually what Tozer prayed. Readers will immediately notice that he addresses God as *Thee* and *Thou*, words we don't often hear anymore. Sometimes the prayers include quotes or paraphrased fragments of Scripture—I have not tried to give references for these, but the reader will certainly recognize them. In certain places where he names individual church members, I have changed these to *brother* or *sister*.

Each chapter starts with short, topical thoughts on prayer that Tozer gave during his Chicago sermons. These additional insights will help the reader better understand the personal thoughts and basis behind the prayer life of A. W. Tozer. All of this material is new, never having been published until now. For readers who are interested, the exact source of the chapter introductions and prayers is listed in the back of the book.

These are not quick, perfunctory prayers—a few words offered because they are somehow required or expected. Instead, they are deeply honest and heartfelt appeals to the resplendent Majesty on High. A. W. Tozer's pastoral prayers have the great potential to help a new generation of pastors to develop their intercessory role as the shepherd of the flock. Each pastor stands (figuratively) at the entrance of their own sheep gate, seeking protection as well as giving warning to the sheep within its walls.

May the Holy Spirit be pleased to use these printed prayers as a possible model or pattern for all sincere worshipers to consider when they themselves are *Approaching the Almighty*.

JESUS CHRIST

I THINK THE GREATEST PRAYER in the world is the unuttered prayer of a great life. I believe that. Jesus prayed. He sent up ejaculatory prayers. He prayed long prayers. He prayed before meals. He prayed in company. He prayed with the people. He prayed alone. He prayed every kind of prayer I suppose there was. But the greatest prayer He ever made was the walk He took from the time He toddled out of Joseph's carpentry shop until they nailed Him on the cross. His life was His greatest prayer.

The Bible says that He pleads for us at the right hand of God the Father Almighty, making intercession for us continually. That has given some people the impression that Jesus Christ is engaged in a perpetual prayer meeting on His knees before the Father, interceding forever. No, His presence there is the most eloquent prayer in all the wide world—that He is there and that we are here, and that He wears our nature and has our shape and looks like us. An angel walking about could see His form and say a man has arrived. A man is in heaven, a man. Sure, a man is there, our man. God's Man, the sample Man, the second Adam. He's there. And His presence there at the right hand of God is the great eloquent prayer for you and me. He bears our names on His hands and on His shoulder and on His breast. And there before the Father, His eloquent presence, is His mighty, efficacious prayer.

Yes, I believe the greatest prayer in the world is the prayer of a life—a life that goes in the right direction. That's not to spiritualize praying, and that is not to give it a mystical turn and relieve us of the privilege and necessity to pray for specific things and expect them. I think we should always be prepared. A man who allows himself to be run down, four days' growth of beard and clothes that are soiled—and then suddenly he has to appear before the King! He's got to do some fast footwork to get ready for that royal appearance. You should be ready all the time.

I think a man is mighty unskillful in prayer if he has to unscramble himself, wash up and get a quick haircut and straighten himself out, trying to look decent as he walks into the presence of God. He should have been like that all the time. Children of God should be presentable all the time. God's people should never need to rush around and get straightened up morally and spiritually to get into the presence of the King. They should live so they can enter that presence without embarrassment, any time. They should have on the robes of presence that would allow them to go in before the King without embarrassment, confident of the things for which they ask.

The Good Shepherd

O Thou Shepherd of Israel, a Shepherd of the sheep, the Lord's my Shepherd, I'll not want. He makes me down to lie in pastures green, He leadeth me the quiet waters by. O Lord, Thou art the Shepherd of Thy sheep, and we're so pleased with the arrangement. We're so glad it worked out that way. We're so glad that Thou didst so have it.

We wouldn't have felt comfortable if Thou hadst made Moses our shepherd. We remember Moses broke some rocks one time, smote another rock, killed a man. We wouldn't have been comfortable if Thou hadst made Elijah our shepherd, because Elijah called down fire.

O Lord Jesus, we're comfortable having Thee as our Shepherd. We're relaxed and restful, for Thou art a good Shepherd, and a great Shepherd, an understanding, sympathetic, loving Shepherd. We thank Thee, Lord Jesus, for being our Shepherd.

We thank Thee for David, but we're glad he's not our shepherd. If he didn't like a man, he ordered his head off. But O Lord, we thank Thee, Thou art our Shepherd.

Now we pray Thee for any who may be lost this night. For Jesus' sake we pray before the lights go out in this building they may have found the Shepherd, because the Shepherd found them. Grant it, for Jesus' sake. Enlarge our hearts. Make us big inside, bigger inside than we are outside. Make us as big as the world. Make us as big as the whole church of God inside—big enough to contain every saint. May Thy mercy be over us now, through Jesus Christ our Lord.

Amen.

Complete in Him

In us, in our flesh, dwelleth no good thing. In our minds dwell no power of persuasion. Without Thee we can do nothing, but with Thee, we can do all things.

So now Father, we turn away as though we were taking an axe away from a little boy and giving it to a man, as though we were shoving aside an amateur, and letting a master sit down to the instrument. We shove aside the man that men know and we invite the man Christ Jesus to speak, who will effectively confirm the Word by the Holy Ghost.

Help us tonight, Lord; tomorrow may be too late! We ask it in Jesus' name.

Amen.

The God-Man

O Lord, O Lord Jesus, our Lord. The great world, sons of Cain, nice people, many of them, friendly people. People who would give a dollar if we got in trouble, would lend us their lawn mower and help us if we got a flat tire, good people. But in religion, they are followers of that man who brought the flowers and didn't bring the blood. Maybe Abel's disposition wasn't as nice as Cain, but he had found the refuge under blood, and he was born of the new Spirit. Then he that was only born once murdered him that was born twice.

O God, we hate to think it—we love people, we love the world. We want to get along with everybody. We wish that we could always nod our head and amen everything that everybody says. We hate to be on the other side. We hate to be stubborn and contentious, but O Jesus, they're saying Thou art a good man. Now there's a saying, they say religion deceives people. So they're fighting it out and they're both wrong. O Christ, Thou art more than the man, Thou art God's Man. Thou art God, Thyself God, begotten of the Father before all ages. Thou art Thyself man, born in Mary, in time. The perfect man and perfect God compounded this night.

O Lord Jesus, we pray that the carelessness and the breeziness might go out of our spirits, that we might wait and know Whose side we're on. O Lord, we take Thy side. Even if it's against our friends, we take Thy side. We own Thee, Lord, to boss us, to tell us what to do, and we promise to obey Thee, O Lord. We would be disciples of Thine, taking the cross and following Thee.

We pray for any who may this night not have taken this

way. We pray for such if they be here. God have mercy, have mercy! Have mercy, O Son of God, have mercy tonight. For the world is very evil, and the times are waxing late, and the judgment is drawing near. We beseech Thee, Lord—pity and spare and forgive and have mercy upon our poor souls. We ask it in Jesus' name.

Amen.

Led by Him

O God our Father, we bless Thy Name, that Thou didst send us help from the sanctuary, out from the heavenly palaces. Down from the lofty heights above, He came. He came to be born under law, to be born of a woman that He might redeem us who were under law, and who by the curse of the law were lost—hopelessly—down to the mud and the blood, down to the shadows and the gloom, down to the tears in the tomb He came. We bless Thy holy Name for sending Him. He came because He wanted to come, but He came because Thou didst send Him. And Father and Son agreed.

We bless Thee, O Triune God. We praise Thee, O blessed Holy Ghost, the conscience of the world that still keeps dimly alive the memory of the world from which we fell. Great God, we do not want Thy wrath to be upon us. We want to have that eternal life which was with Thee. We pray, help tonight that there might not be one goes out of here who has not received the Son, who has not obeyed the Son, who has not now taken the Son and believed the Son.

O Son of Man, we hear Thy voice. Son of God, we see Thy light. Wilt Thou grant, we pray, that as we go from this place tonight, we may go driven by the hard, overwhelming force of logic to Jesus Christ the Lord? To know that there's nothing on our level, ancient or modern, that can help us remotely, but only He who came from above, only Jesus. Blessed be the name Jesus. We pray Thee, help us love that name and follow whithersoever He goeth.

Help these friends who listen tonight. We thank Thee for the privilege of speaking to them. O Lord we pray, send them out with a bit of another world on their hearts, a yearning, a longing and aspiration, that they may open wide the gates of their soul and receive the Lord Christ in and rest in Him and trust Him and know that even now in the Spirit, they can be raised out of the valley. And finally, that He's coming, taken out for good. And the valley itself, transformed no longer into the valley, from the valley of death, but now of life. For the knowledge of the Lord shall cover the earth as the waters cover the sea. We pray in Jesus' name.

Amen.

Adopted

God and Father of our Lord Jesus, we thank Thee this hour. Thou hast not left us orphans. Thou hast not allowed us to wander into the serpent-infested valleys and left us there. But Thou hast allured us and wooed us, and even there hast placed a door.

Wherever we are, there's a way out and a way in from that spot. Thou hast secured us in Thy grace. Thou hast sent Thy Son, Jesus to die, to rise, to live, to plead—and to be for us, Advocate above, as Savior by the throne of love. And while He's there and we're here, the door is within touch.

We bless Thee. We will not despair. We will not give up. We will not surrender to the suggestions of the enemy. We will dare to believe that with every temptation, Thou wilt make a way of escape. Thou wilt turn our tin into silver and our silver into gold, and Thou wilt give us the garments of praise for the garments of heaviness. Bless Thou the Word spoken this morning. We ask it in the name of Jesus Christ our Lord.

Amen.

Our Greatest Treasure

O Lord, we're more concerned that if everything be all right with us, now, and in the day of our death, or at the coming of Thy Son. We're more concerned that if we stand well in religion, that we have a reputation among the saints. We're more concerned, Lord, that things be now right with us. Oh, we thank Thee, Lord Jesus. Thou didst say to such poor, world-wanderers as we are, "If ye become my disciples and follow me, and go on and become disciples, indeed ye shall know the truth and the truth shall make you free. And if the Son sets you free, you shall be free indeed, for I am the Light of the World and he that follows me shall never walk in darkness, but shall have the light of life."

Thank Thee, Lord—there need be no concern, need be no doubts, need be no worries. We can know that we're following Thee. As we walk in the light, as Thou art in the light, we have fellowship with Thee and with one another, and the blood of Jesus Christ, Thy Son, cleanses us from all sin. This is a greater treasure than all the gold of Ophir or the diamonds of Africa— more to be desired is it than all jewels, all rubies, all the corn and wheat and all the granaries of the world.

So, we seek tonight to know and be sure that we're not only descendants of the Reformers, but true sons of their faith and obedience. Whatever our denomination is, we're not only in the tradition of our denomination, but that we have the spiritual experiences of those who in other days brought those denominations into existence by their faith.

Thank Thee for every true Methodist. Thank Thee for every holy Presbyterian. Thank Thee for every godly Baptist. Thank

Thee for every happy Nazarene. Thank Thee, O Lord, for every blessed, heart-happy Quaker. Thank Thee for every man and woman of God—whatever denomination—that loves Thee tonight, and we feel we're a part of their fellowship. But oh, save us, we pray Thee, from the tragedy and snare of entrenched privilege, of vested interests, believing everything's all right, because we're descended from parents that are all right. Great God, save us from this!

Now, we trust Thee, that Thou wouldst send us out from this church with a quiet, certain, sure gaze at the Light of the World, meekly disclaiming all self-righteousness, humbly denying ourselves, willingly taking the cross, sorry for all that is imperfect and wrong, glad for the blood that cleanses, grateful for the grace that pardons. And remember sin no more, forever. Blessed be Thy name.

Amen.

Trusting with Confidence

O Lord Jesus, Thou knowest prophetic teachers are not agreed, and we don't claim tonight. We're not even going to pray tonight for the moment, for universal revival, though we think it's theoretically possible. But Father, we think everybody's agreed on personal revival. That it's entirely possible for the coldest, most barren, gloomiest, most defeated Christian, within a few hours' time, to move into a place of victory and fruitfulness and power and optimism and happiness, such as they've never dreamed could be theirs.

We believe it's entirely possible for a church that has dragged for years, and suddenly come alive, as though Thou hadst said, "Let there be light and there was light." Thou hadst said, "Let the church bring forth," and lo, it was so. We believe this Lord, and we want it for ourselves. We want it for this church. We want it for these who will listen tonight. We want a personal revival in each heart. We want the church revival that will melt us all in one, who had the individual revival.

O God, we beseech Thee, give us tonight vision to see it, courage to take advantage of it, and faith to believe it. Now that Thou would revive Thy Work. That Thou would move in and the eyes of men shall see the Glory of the Lord. O Lord Jesus, Thou Glory-bringer, Thou Joy-dispenser, Thou Physician of souls, Thou Son of Righteousness with healing in Thy wings, Thou Star of the East, the horizon adorned Him, Thou bringer of Good Tidings.

O Lord Jesus, we've shut Thee out so long. Thou hast knocked at our doors so long and we've been asleep, or we've been preoccupied. Forgive Thee, Lord, forgive. Forgive those who listen. Forgive tonight. Forgive us for failing Thee there. And give us a strong and courageous purpose, and beginning now, we will straighten up.

Beginning now, we will fill up the hollow places and begin to do the things we've stopped doing or never did. And we'll smooth down the bumps, those ugly humps that indicate the presence of things committed and done that ought not to be done. Father, we'll stop doing them. We'll smooth the way by repentance and humility and meekness in spirit. Great God, help us.

Our High Priest

Now Father, we pray Thy blessing upon us. Oh, we scatter from this little building to so many places. So many responsibilities, obligations, callings, and back to school for many. Oh, we pray that we'll go with confidence that we're not orphans of the storm. That we're not bits of matter, animated for a period, floating in space. That we're sons and daughters of a God who's got His eye on every one of us and knows our name and number and face, and the High Priest carries our name on His shoulder and on His breast and on His forehead before the presence of God. Before the face of the Father, stands our great High Priest, and we need no merit of saints. We need nothing but the merit of the great High Priest.

We thank Thee we can enter boldly into the throne of grace and receive mercy and grace to help in time of need. For He knoweth our infirmities, and feels all the pinch and pressure of our weaknesses, for He was Himself man and walked among us. Send us out with great hope and encouragement. Send these young people back to school, chins up and knees bent and eyes bright knowing that the Lord is on their side and grace, infinite, matchless grace is greater than all their sins.

Send us back to service and out to our neighbors, confidently expecting that we shall see the gifts of the Spirit restored to this church. And that we shall see the mighty power of a risen Christ operating in this church. We ask these things in His name.

Amen.

Clarity and Security

O Lord, we thank Thee that Thou didst come to rescue us on a life raft, ready to perish, shark fins breaking the water all about us, Thou didst come walking upon the sea. Thou didst say, "Be not afraid, it is I."

We thank Thee, O Thou Shepherd, Thou pilot in Galilee. Thou Savior of mankind. Wilt Thou bless us and help us? Save us, we pray Thee, from the fogginess and muddiness of our thinking. Clarify us in our eyesight, poor eyesight, on blind eyes. And may we see the sharp, clear line that distinguishes those who are from those who are not. Those who will from those who won't. We thank Thee, Lord, for everyone that will, and thank Thee for the security afforded us in Christ by the old rugged cross.

Now, bless us for the afternoon. Give us an afternoon of relaxation and meditation. Save us from thinking, saying, or doing anything that would tend to cloud up the sky above us. And bring us back tonight, we pray, and add greatly to our numbers as Thou has been doing these nights. And may we make some real progress in the Christian life today. In Christ's name.

Amen.

Come and Rest

Blessed Lord Jesus, blessed Lord Jesus, ruler of all nature. O Thou of God and man, the Son. How we love Thee. How we praise Thee. How we bless Thee. In our folly and shame and infamy we were never at rest, and we sought eagerly to satisfy ourselves. When it was over, it wasn't satisfying. It still left a hollow there. A broken cistern, we found nothing in it but lizards and dust.

But we thank Thee we heard the voice of Jesus say, "Come unto me and rest." We came and we laid our head upon Thy breast and we heard the voice of Jesus say, "I am this dark world's Light; look unto me, Thy morn shall rise, and all Thy day be bright." I came to Jesus and I found in Him my star, my sun, and in the light of life I'll walk till traveling days are done.

O Jesus, Thou art so much that we don't know how to pray even. We know not how to pray. We stand before what Thou art, as a little boy before a mountain. Vast, illimitable, huge, and awesome. Thou art all that we want and need. Thou art calling us to Thyself.

Please don't let anybody lay his head on a pillow tonight until he has turned from the folly of the fool to the wisdom of the just. And has sought to become another man indeed, and be born again by faith in the shed blood and atonement which Christ made. Amen and amen.

Amen.

Ready for Him

O God, we thank Thee Thou didst not forget us in the night. We thank Thee Thou didst send Thine only be-gotten Son, God of God, Light of Light, very God of very God, begotten, not made. Being of one substance with the Father, who created heaven and earth. We thank Thee that He came. He grew. He died. He rose. He lives now at the right hand of God, the Father Almighty. We thank Thee that from His place of vantage there, all power is His.

And we bless Thee, O Lord God, we bless Thee, that we are not pensively looking back tonight to a manger and a virgin, but upward and upward where the stars are turning. Upward where the holy angels veil their faces. Upward where the seraphim hide their feet and their hands and their faces as they cry "Holy, holy, holy is the Lord God Almighty. Heaven and earth are full of His glory."

And Lord, Thou hast there our names. Thou hast our names on Thy hands engravened and on Thy bosom and on Thy shoulders and in Thy heart. Thou art there our Advocate above, our Savior, by the throne of love. We praise Thee tonight, Lord Jesus, that nothing can change that, nothing. Nothing can take it away. Nothing can rob us, Lord, nothing. We thank Thee, Lord God, this evening that it is well with us because we have been touched by the wand of Him who rules heaven and earth and at whose feet soon the earth and the hell and the heaven above shall kneel and declare that He is Lord to the glory of God the Father.

Wilt Thou help us this evening, Lord? Bless us greatly. Bless the music and the message of truth which shall follow. And grant we pray Thee, O Lord, we may go out from here determined with our jaws tight shut and our feet set in the way of Zion and our face like a flint, that come what may, we'll follow Jesus. Not only when the snows come and the green holly tell us it is Christmas, but all through the long drag of February and March and over into the heat of summer. And regardless of what kind of weather nor what season of the year, follow the Lord Jesus Christ steadily along, until we shall be glorified together.

Graciously bless us now tonight we pray. Give us, we pray,

receptive hearts to receive all of the truth that will come down from Thy throne to us. Not only for ourselves we pray, but for all the churches, Lord, everywhere, all the churches, that Christ may be magnified in our mortal bodies and in our lives until He come. We ask it in Jesus' holy name.

Amen.

BLOOD OF CHRIST

"Ye have not, because ye asked not" (James 4:2). There is a penalty for prayerlessness. You could have had it if you had asked for it. You're not asking for it and therefore, you're not getting it. How little we have may be the result of how little we ask. More asking means more getting. Less asking means less getting. "Ye have not, because ye asked not." That's the penalty of prayerlessness.

"Ye ask, and receive not, because ye ask amiss, that ye may consume it upon your lusts" (James 4:3). There's the penalty of selfishness. To ask selfishly that I might have it to consume it upon my lusts is to make it impossible for God to answer. And then, ask and ye shall receive. There's the reward of faithfulness. The penalty of prayerlessness, ye ask and receive not because ye ask amiss, the penalty of selfishness. And ask and ye shall receive the reward of faithfulness.

It is important to know that prayer is not simply something that religious-minded people mumble, but it's a science and it's an art. It is a skill to be learned by the grace of God. It is a privilege to be enjoyed. It is an authority to be wielded and a right you and I have in the blood of the Lamb. We can go to God and ask what we will and it shall be done unto us.

Do you believe that? Will you then practice it a little more than you have been? Will you do it? Will you take it on yourself? Will you dare to go to God? If you shouldn't have something, don't ask for it. Don't want it. Stop wishing. God's poor sheep—wishing, wishing, wishing—like the farmer that sits on the front porch and wishes for ten acres of golden corn. And he calls his wife and says, "Mae, would you please join me in wishing for ten acres of golden corn?" So she joins him.

She says, "George, I think that we ought to call in our neighbors. I think there's power in numbers. Let's call in our neighbors." So she goes to the old phone and rings three times, and the neighbor answers and she says, "Come on over. George and I are sitting on the front porch wishing for ten acres of golden corn!"

Pretty soon they have a front porch full of people all sitting there wishing for corn. I know it's ridiculous. I know it—but a lot of God's children are doing the same thing. They're wishing for things. Stop wishing. If you ought to have it, pray and you'll get it.

God won't do what you can do. And there's no use for you to try to do what only God can do. And if we can get untangled on this one thing, so we're not trying to do what only God can do, and not asking God to do what we ought to go and do.

Precious Blood

Dear Lord Jesus, we say with Thy servant David, "Our hope is in Thee." We say with Peter, "Lord, to whom shall we go? Where, Lord, can we go? Thou hast the words of eternal life."

Lord Jesus, there's science, psychology, and learning and religion and preoccupation, but not one of them affords a hiding place against the storm. Not one of them has a fountain where we can clean our souls, not one. Lord, Thou alone art our hope. Thou art our hope.

We bless Thee. We worship Thee. We praise Thee. We magnify Thee for Thy precious blood, the blood that cleansed Paul (a murderer), John Newton, Mel Trotter, Jerry McCauley, Billy Sunday, and ten thousand times ten thousand whose names are never known in public, but who were sinners deep, died, and lost, but were washed by holy blood, cleansed, renewed, and are now happy in Jesus, O Lord—the many who have gone on, and there are many who are still here.

How we thank Thee for that perfect gospel. We don't apologize for it. We don't even try to understand it. We only know that simple trust in the precious blood makes the soul clean and brings us into knowledge of eternal life through Jesus Christ the Savior.

We pray Thee for these friends who are here tonight. O God, let them not go out untouched with thoughts of holy things. Let them not go out uninfluenced by impulses of the Spirit, let them not go out as they came in, but sobered and thoughtful. We don't want them to go out heavy-hearted nor gloomy. There's no gloom nor heaviness in the cheerful call of the Holy Ghost. But we pray Thee that they go out serious and sober and thoughtful, saying to themselves, *I'm here for a little time and then I'll go. What am I waiting around for? Why all this postponement? Why this loitering? Why this tarrying?*

O Lord Jesus, some of us were never saved in church at all. Some of us hunted an attic room or a basement room or a park. Or somewhere, there in loneliness, we poured out our grief and raised our Bethel and met Thee. Lord, we pray if there be some here tonight, that before the midnight bells toll, that they might have found Thee, that they might find the Savior.

Bless Thou the saved tonight. Lord Jesus, these who are unsaved and bring them in. For the young folks that are friendly, nice kids, but O God, so far from Thee and their feelings and emotions and impulses and ambitions, so horribly carnal, yet they say they're saved. We pray for them. O Christ, may they go on to perfection. May they leave the first beginnings of the things of the Lord and put behind in the world and under their feet, the carnal things of flesh, and rise on Jacob's Ladder. And seek the highlands and the pure, sun-kissed hilltops, where the air is rare and sweet embracing, but where they can see over Jordan and behold, the bright tops of the City of God. Grant this, we pray, for Jesus' holy sake.

Amen.

Broken for Us

Father, we pray Thy blessing upon this Word. Now, as we enter our Communion service, we pray that in utter humility and meekness and humbleness of spirit, we may be, and insist upon and being, what Thou dost declare us to be. And we may deduce from Thy own characterizations of us what kind of holy men and women we ought to be, showing forth the praises of Him who brought us out of darkness and into His marvelous light. Take away all bitterness, all resentfulness, all this disquietude, all discontent. And bring us, we pray Thee, into mental and spiritual harmony as we think together of the shed blood in the broken body. In Jesus' name.

Amen.

Limitless Redemption

O Jesus, our Lord, Thy blood had and has limitless, unique, infinite value and it's power. Its purchasing power, its power to achieve before the bar of God, its power to redeem is infinite and unique and limitless. One drop of Thy blood has infinite value. And all our sins are finite by comparison. All the sins of all the world couldn't weigh over against a drop of Thy blood for where sin abounded, grace does much more abound. And whereas we sin with limit, Thou didst die without limit. Thy blood was shed without limit for us.

Please God, grant that if you have to chasten us and whip us, if you have to rob us and strip us—and like Job, put us on an ash pile—don't let anybody here tonight lose his soul. Don't let anybody here tonight give to the devil, who doesn't deserve anything. Not the valuable self for which Jesus died.

O God, we pray, grant that these friends may invest their lives. Give them to Thee. Give them over, and turn them over and say, "Take my life and let it be consecrated, Lord, to Thee. Take my hands, take my feet, take my lips, take my tongue, take my eyes and ears. Take me Lord, take me and make me Thine."

Grant we may be invested, rather than wasted and spent. Invest Lord. May these investments, may we invest ourselves, not at six percent nor eight percent nor twelve percent, but a percent so often compounded and so infinitely multiplied that the angels couldn't keep the books, if we invest ourselves.

God, hear us, for these who listened tonight and have lived it. Send us out determined that if it means the loss of friends and money and every earthly thing, we're going to invest ourselves in the cross and give ourselves to the Christ, and follow the Lamb wherever He goes. This we ask in Jesus' name.

Amen.

The Blood Applied

Dear Lord Jesus, we pray for these who said *pray for me*. O Lord Jesus, Satan hath desired to have these that he might sift them like wheat, and he wants them. Thou didst buy them by Thy blood. Thou didst give Thy life for them when Thy soul was made an offering for sin. Thou didst give Thyself as a ransom because You loved them so. Satan is trying to win them and they're caught in the middle.

O Lord, we pray, that they may this very night, now while there's opportunity, believe and dare to believe that the blood of Jesus Christ cleanses from all sin. Make them willing now to look back to see the blood applied. Help us all, Father, help us all. Don't let any of us be deceived. Don't let me, or the board members, or the Sunday school teachers, or any missionaries who might be present, or any of these who witnessed and testified on this street or in jails or hospitals—don't let any of us be deceived, Lord! We want to know the whole truth, now and have it over with, so we can look up to heaven and say, "Arise, my soul, arise." Great God, help these people, every last one of them.

Infinite Merit

O God, with these refreshing words ringing in our hearts, we now approach Thee in prayer. We pray that Thou will accept our gratitude. We're grateful that we're alive. We're grateful we ever were born. We're grateful that having been born and having sinned and gone astray, we were followed by the Good Shepherd until He found us and laid us on His shoulder and brought us home rejoicing. Father, for all of this, we are thankful. I cannot express it. Words will not express the feelings of the heart. But we give Thee at least, O God, what we can in a bouquet of words, as a thank offering, tell Thee that we're grateful that we were brought into the world. And then, brought into the new world and born again and renewed by the blessed Holy Ghost through Jesus Christ our Lord.

Father, we're here to hear Thy Word, to refresh our hearts by song, to pray, to worship Thee above all, and to make our gifts unto Thee. Now, we pray we may do these things in a manner, becoming redeemed sinners, and in a manner becoming Thee, the high and holy God. Father, forgive and overlook, we pray, our ignorance and our lack of divine etiquette—our inability and our failure to know just how to act in the presence of the King. But we're learning and, Lord, we will learn. We're here this morning that we might learn. So we pray Thee, overlook our awkwardness and forgive our ignorance. And accept our love and our faith and our worship through the blood of Jesus that makes everything all right.

Now, we ask Thee, Lord, for our upcoming missionary convention which will begin in a matter of weeks, we pray that we might be spiritually prepared and arrive at it in a state of spiritual alertness and humility, that we can see our greatest convention this year. And for the Council that lies yet before us here in the city and for each facet of the church's work and for all that Thou has put in our hands to do, we beseech Thee, that we may do it well, and not deceitfully or carelessly.

We pray for our sick that Thou wilt heal them and that Thou, God, wilt comfort them where they are. Remember the bereaved in the trouble throughout our broad society. Please remember Thy work in the earth. Remember those doors that are temporarily closed and hear the prayers of thousands that they might be opened again, places like China. Lord, we don't give it up. We believe that Thou art the Sovereign God and yet, those several hundred million people will hear the gospel of Christ. We are trusting Thee as we wait in Thy presence this morning, through Christ Jesus our Lord.

Amen.

Riches of His Blood

O God, through Jesus Christ our Lord, we thank Thee for Thy suffering humanity. We can't rise, we can't rise, Lord, where we're born averse and clay, and we've got bones and we can't rise, Lord. We're hugged down to earth by gravitational pull. And we can't rise and soar off. But, O Lord Jesus, we can crawl into Thy suffering humanity. Hide ourselves there where the blood runs, and there we can begin. There we can enter. There we can find cleansing. Then, Thou will lead us onward and upward, but we'll begin with our humanity.

Thy blood, Jesus, Thy blood, Thy righteousness, Thy glory are my heavenly bliss. In Thee didst flaming world arrayed with joy, shall I lift up my head? O Lord Jesus, please help these, whatever they want. However high the flight they want to take, however deep they want to go, however far they want to travel— help them, we pray Thee, to enter by the cross, by the blood, and to take the victory of that blood, the liberty of that blood, the freedom of that blood, the strength and power of that blood, and to go on and on through that blood. O Lord Jesus, we bless Thee for shedding that blood for us.

Now, once more, we pray for all who followed Thee in baptism tonight, who have said, "We've put the world behind us. We enter into a new life. We rise in newness of life. We're not under law, but under grace, and we walk no longer in the flesh, but in the Spirit." For these others now, we pray for them each one, O God. Oh, we pray Thee that Thou would help them to learn the lesson and repent, and continue repenting and putting under their feet the lion and the dragon—trampling every bad habit under their feet, and putting behind them every wickedness until they're clean as clean can be. Until the blood of Christ has made them holy. Fill them, we pray, with the Holy Ghost.

Lead us out from here now and give us safe conduct to our

homes. Bless us over these streets. May Thy mercy and grace be with us through Christ our Lord.

Amen.

Remembering His Death

Father, bless Thou the Word. Prepare our hearts as we try to obey Thy Son the best we know how. Dear heavenly Father, we have been told by Thy Son, our Savior, that we were to break the bread and drink of this same cup. And Thy children down the years have disagreed about how it was to be done and have disagreed about the frequency of it, and they even disagreed about the meaning of it. We can't bow before Thee this day and tell Thee, Lord, that we know it all. We don't, but we want to do the best we know how, and in meekness of humility we want to eat and drink, remembering the Lord's death until He comes. And if we can't do it wisely, help us to do it humbly, and if we don't have the right theological notion about it, then help us to have humility that makes up for it, and the tender faith and love.

Give us the gratitude that weeps inwardly over the blood He shed in the body, the beautiful thirty-three-year-old, beautiful body, unscarred, unmarred, never sick, handsome, but broken for us. Help us, we pray, to have great gratitude. And then, if we don't have it often enough or if tradition and the passing of the years has dimmed it until we may be off a little somewhere or other—we'll be on, and it will be right, and we'll be accepted because Thou dost accept love and faith even if our heads don't understand. So wilt Thou bless the fellowship around the table this morning? We ask it through Jesus Christ, Thy Son.

Amen.

Altar of Sacrifice

O Jesus, Jesus, Jesus! Thou didst come down and was born of the Virgin Mary. The Father gave Thee a body they could drive nails in and put a spear in. Thou wast crucified by the men Thou didst love. Nailed on a tree by the very ones Thou didst come to save.

And Thou didst say, if the world hated you, it hated Me first before it hated you. Brace yourselves and get ready and expect it, and preach the gospel to every creature. Make disciples out of all nations. And there will be a minority group, small numbered, who will believe in Me. Wicked men, seducers shall wax worse and worse until the end come.

O Lord Jesus, here we are—moving on, moving on with the irresistible motion toward the end, toward judgment. Great God, this evening, we pray, don't let us be careless. Don't let us go on as men are going on, even as religious people are going on, ignoring realities. We pray Thee, Lord, help us not to be like the peacock to raise our feathers and make them stand on end, to make ourselves look five times bigger than we are. Help us, we pray, to know how little we are and to know how bad we are and to know how desperately we need the blood of the Lamb and how terribly we need the forgiving love of God.

Oh help us, and send us out from here sobered and humbled and with our eyes sharpened and brightened, that we can look past the fog and see the mountains that we won't crash into them. Give us, we pray Thee, eyes that can see through, and ears that know the sound of the Shepherd's Voice. Give us a sense of smell that recognizes the difference and knows what is right and what is wrong. Save us, we pray Thee, from make-believe and pretense. And let us get back to Calvary and down to reality and where the witness of the Spirit whispers within, and tells us we were born of God.

Bless Thy church, Lord, Thy church. We thank Thee that Thou hast seven thousand that have not bowed the knee to Baal and no doubt in this day many more than that. Oh, bless that seven thousand, Lord. We beseech Thee this night, bless every true saint of God of whatever denomination or color around the whole world, every true one who's identified himself with a rejected Savior, willing to be rejected till he's accepted at last, leaning on the arm of his Beloved. Help us now as we wait upon Thee for a little, in Jesus' holy name.

Amen.

Cleansed by the Lamb

Now, Lord, we thank Thee that we believe this with everything in us. We believe that living, we believe, we'll believe it's Thine. And we'll believe it when our feeble faltering voice can no more sing it, we'll believe it and whisper it, that the precious blood of Jesus can cleanse from all sin. Father we won't grieve Thy heart by trying to explain, or rejecting because we can't explain it.

We are believers. And we have this faith as an organ of knowledge, and we believe and therefore we know that the blood of the dying Lamb shall make His church white and clean. She shall join Him and be led into the presence of the Father with exceeding joy in those days that are just ahead of us, out yonder. In the light of all this, how small this world seems and how little and how poor, and how little it matters about all the details that trouble.

Now, as we go, dismiss us, we beseech Thee, with Thy good favor and Thy kind hand. Smile at us as we go, through Jesus Christ. We can know and feel and be assured that we're living in heaven, even while we're on earth. May grace and mercy be upon us through Jesus Christ our Lord.

Amen.

WORD OF GOD

I WOULD LIKE TO GIVE A DEFINITION of prayer which I got from Miguel de Molinos, the great Spanish saint who said that prayer is an ascent or elevation of the mind to God. Very simple, isn't it? Prayer is an ascent of the mind to God. It is an elevation of the mind. Saying that it is an ascent simply means that it ascends to God. But saying that it is an elevation of the mind indicates that there's something you've got to do to elevate it. God is above all creatures and the soul cannot see Him or converse with Him unless you raise yourself above all creatures, and that's what Molinos said, prayer is the elevation of the soul, the flight of the soul, of the mind to God. Now that's a good definition of prayer, but there are also some biblical texts that say some specific things as well about prayer.

The first one, James 5:16, says that prayer is a potent thing, that it "availeth much." I would cite those words, "availeth much," as constituting a terrific understatement for the Old Testament and the New Testament combine to teach and demonstrate how much prayer availeth. And the Holy Ghost Himself labors, in this same James, the fifth chapter, to show us by example how much prayer availeth by citing Elijah's ability to turn heaven off and on, that is, the clouds, to make them rain or not rain as he pleased. That's one statement, prayer availeth much.

Also in James 4:2 and 3 we read that sometimes we do not have the advantage of prayer for one of two reasons: either we have failed to ask or we have asked selfishly. And therefore we do not have the benefits that prayer could bring. That's the negative side. Prayer availeth much, but you're not getting much availed. Therefore, it could be because we have failed to ask or, having asked, we've done so selfishly.

Then our Lord in Luke 18:1 says that nevertheless, in spite of the difficulties and the problems that are before us, "we ought always to pray." And in this passage, as far as I know, it's the only parable of our Lord that starts out by telling what it's going to teach. This is one parable that none of the commentators ever quarrel over. Mostly, they quarrel in a good-natured, nice way, often disagreeing over what the parables teach. But this one they can't disagree over because we're told, He spake a parable unto them to this end. In other words, before He told us the parable, He told us what the parable would teach. He made a statement and illustrated it with a story—a short one, but a story. And He said, "The reason I tell you this story is that men ought always to pray and not to faint."

God Almighty not only commands that we ought always to pray, His Word confirms its potency and the benefits to those who do so.

Plainly Speaking

O Christ, everything seems so simple and we, like the Jews, are looking for miracles. We, like the Greeks, are looking for wisdom when it's all so very simple. "If you will amend your doings and obey My voice, then I will cleanse you whiter than snow and make you as white as wool. Ye shall eat of the good of the land." Father, it's so simple. We beseech Thee, help us to see it.

We beseech Thee that we may not foolishly cast away these great gems of truth. We pray Thee tonight, our Father, that we may not fail to hear Thee speaking to us when Thou art speaking so plainly.

God, bless this people. It's hot here tonight, and the people have listened with patience. O God, Holy Spirit, we beseech Thee, drive Thy merciful arrows so deep into their hearts that they will not be able to pull them out ever until they come to Calvary's fountain where they are cleansed and forgiven and healed and the old wound of conviction is drawn and cleansed and healed. Help us as we wait upon Thee.

Amen.

Gracious Promises

O ur Father, we this hour draw near in thoughts to Thee. We have been near to Thee, but our thoughts sometimes stray, so we would draw in our thoughts this hour. We would call in our thoughts that roam abroad and center them upon Thee, on Thy Holy Son, and upon the Holy Spirit, and upon Thy universal church, and upon the heavenly places and heavenly things.

We thank Thee for Thy severe, yet gracious Word, for Thy promises, for Thyself, who makes the promises good. And we thank Thee for the fellowship of Thy children.

Now, Father, today a great many, an unbelievably large percentage of the fellowship here are away some place, vacation, traveling, attending some strange church in some strange town. And we pray for them, every one. Lord, they're our sheep. They're Thy sheep, keep them. Let nothing happen to them, either morally or physically. Keep them and restore them again to this fellowship.

Please bless now all the conventions over the states and up into Canada. Let mercy be over all summer Bible conferences. In and out of our society, bless every man who stands to preach. Great God, make us better than we are. Give humility, simplicity, and a thirst after Thyself. Save us from professionalism. Save us from seeking the immunity of the pulpit. Save us, we pray Thee, O God, from being false prophets, running when we are not sent, repeating that which is only rote. Send us prophets and teachers and holy men who shall speak as they're moved by the Holy Ghost to declare the inspired Word of God.

Bless Thy work throughout the earth. We pray for our country. Gracious Father, remember our country. Give us optimism. Give us hope, we pray. Give us courage to pray for a nation that seems to care nothing for itself. And yet, turn us back to Thee, O God, and in wrath, remember mercy.

Bless us here today as we worship before Thee, O Lord. Give us childlike hearts, simple souls, transparent minds, and a faith that will not shrink but will mount up and gaze and gaze on Thee. We see Thee and behold Thee in Thy goodness, in Thy grace. Remember our sick—there are quite a number of them. We pray for this brother's operation. Remember, we pray, some who've recently had various kinds of surgery. Remember those who are kept home with the sick.

Be gracious to us, O Lord, and think upon us and fulfill Thy Word which says, "I know the thoughts that I think toward you, thoughts of peace and not of evil." Think upon us, O God, we pray, graciously and with peace. We ask it in the name of Thy Son, Jesus Christ our Lord.

Amen.

The Eternal Word

O God, we thank Thee for the Truth, the helpful, encouraging, wondrous Truth that illuminates our minds, encourages our hearts, and cheers us in discouragement. We thank Thee that we feel Thy heartbeat in it and we feel the warmth of Thy presence in it. We sense Thy great care and lovingkindness as we read together and hear Thee say, oh, that Thou wouldest. And it makes our hearts want to respond to Thee and say, "O Lord, we will. We will follow Thee, O God, and we'll obey Thee."

Speak Thou in the secret place of thunder. That deep call unto the deep at the noise of Thy waterspouts. And we pray Thee, deliver our hands from the burdens and our shoulders from the yoke, and lay upon us rather Thine own easy yoke. For Thy yoke is easy and Thy burden is light and Thy commandments are not grievous.

We pray for this our worship, O God. Drive far from us dull-witted care. Take far away from us the corrosive acids that eat into our souls, and pour on the oil that heals and perfumes and makes fragrant. God, help us. We have come another week on our way. Another seven days have passed. The sun has risen and set. The wind has blown from its gaze and we are near home.

God, we pray Thee, give us worshiping hearts today: hearts that will worship the Father, the source of our being, the foundation upon which we rest. Eternal Word that speaketh always to us, help now, Lord.

Remember the churches that are gathering. Remember the country. Remember Thy work. Remember the nations of the earth. Remember Thy promises unto the fathers and Thy promises through Jesus Thy Son and through the apostles that we have believed, and fulfill them in their turn. Remember Thou, O my God, Thy covenants, sealed with holy blood, and do what Thou hast promised to do. We trust Thee as we wait. In the precious name of Jesus.

Amen.

Truthful Words

O Lord, our Lord, we thank Thee the Father gave Thee to us. And the Father said Thou, O Christ, art His Son in whom He was well pleased, "mine Elect in whom my soul delighteth." O Christ, we love Thee! Thou knowest we do. We love Thy sweet name. Every name Thou bearest is dear to us. Everything Thou didst ever do is dear to us.

Every word You ever said is dear to us. We want to know the whole truth, now while we can do something about it. We want to know whether we're victims of an emotional attachment to an abstraction—or whether it be we are followers of Thine and obedient to Thy Word, Thy wonderful Word spoken to us, telling us what to do and how to live, and giving us the power by the indwelling Spirit. What Thou dost command, Thou dost also enable, and every commandment carries its own enabling in it.

O Jesus, we pray Thee for this people to listen tonight. Save us from the heresy of disjointed Christianity. Save us, we pray Thee our God, from having our feet so far from our heads that our feet never get going. Put Thy love in our hand and in our feet and in our wills so that our love will result in obedience and we will obey Thee and be ready always to do Thy Word and follow Thy sayings, and take up our cross daily, deny ourselves, and follow along behind Thee like little Christian on his way to the Celestial City, looking away to the rising light. Great God, help these people to see. Graciously bless us. In Jesus' name.

Amen.

Illuminated Word

O our Savior, we're bringing a series of sermons to an end, but we're not bringing to an end our thirst, our determination, our purpose—that we are pressing on, that we've got the hilltop in view, and that's without any righteousness of our own, but having that righteousness which is of God by faith. We press forward toward the prize.

We thank Thee, Lord God, that there are experiences of power and of liberation and of deliverance. There is a passing out of Egypt, and a passing across the Jordan into the Holy Land and moving up and moving in and the driving out of the inhabitants and the taking over. All these are before us. We pray that Thou will put a quiet but steadfast purpose within our hearts, all of our hearts, that we may seek Thy face, determined that whatever the cost, we will serve Thee.

We pray, our Lord Jesus, that Thou wilt put the right books into the hands of the hungry hearted, and get them aimed in the right direction, and let light fall upon the Word. Bring truth to sight. Save us, we beseech Thee, from the tradition of the elders. And may we, with a burst of spiritual imagination and aspiration and longing, leap forward, instead of, as the world gets worse, the church gets cooler and colder and religion gets further from New Testament standards.

We pray for those who've listened and these that were present here tonight, we may set our hearts, like a flint, determined that we're going to be as Lot in Sodom, as Daniel in Babylon, as the saints in Caesar's household, as the Methodists in a wicked and adulterous England, and as all of those have had to be—live above our environment, live above our religious environment, take our stand above it, and rest in Thee. Gracious Father, grant this, we beseech Thee. This we ask in the name of Jesus our Lord. Amen.

The Word Fulfilled

Now we walk out on Thy Word, as Peter walked out on the water. We pray, help us not to look down at our feet but help us to look away up to Thee and expect Thy Word to be fulfilled in us, as it was written for Israel and will be prophetically fulfilled in that great Day, but also spiritually fulfilled within all

Thy children that dare to trust Thee and dare to believe.

Now, we pray Thy blessing on us this evening. Father, we think of this great city. The darkness that has settled down tonight is symbolic of the darkness that's upon the city, on the hearts of the people of this city—lust and hate and greed and drunkenness and worldliness and unbelief. Lord, it lies on us and can't be overstated. Darkness shall cover the earth and gross darkness the people. But it's written, Lord, that unto them that sat in the shadow of death, light has shined.

So, wilt Thou shine upon us, O Lighthouse, this night? Shine Thou upon us. Lord, we're not worthy of it. We belong to the darkness too. But we sometimes also walked in darkness after the course of this world. O God, let light shine down in this congregation tonight. That light shine down, we pray Thee, over on the north side and down further south and out west and in the east and all over the city where congregations meet, big and little congregations, to hear the Word preached.

Honor the Word, we pray Thee, O God, and bless the people and upset Satan. Give him, we pray Thee, a jar tonight. Set him back on his heels. Drive out this obscene rebel and turn the people loose, O God, and set them free that they may walk as servants of the Most High God.

Bless our country and the world, and pity and spare tonight, O Lord God, in that strange, weird place they call the United Nations building and other places where men meet to try to keep peace. God, bless Thou the nations of the world. Bless Thou, we pray Thee, among the foreign missionaries and missionary movements and their boards and independent missionaries, that are out trying to preach the gospel. O Lord God, give, we pray Thee, a big help tonight, every place over the earth, and be with us here. To Thee we'll give praise to Jesus Christ our Lord.

Amen.

Words That Shine

Our Heavenly Father, we are encouraged and refreshed and renewed just by hearing these sacred words read. For Thou hast said that it is by Thy Word that all things were and came to be. Thou didst speak and it was done. Thou didst command and it stood forth. Thou didst send Thy Word and healed them. Thou didst speak and Lazarus came out of the grave. By Thy Word Thou upholdest the universe. And by Thy Word, Thou art carrying out Thy eternal purposes, purposed in Christ Jesus before the world began.

We bless Thee. We worship Thee. We praise Thee this morning, Father, Son and Holy Spirit. We bless Thee. We thank Thee, Father, that Thou hast turned our hearts upward toward Thee. Thou hast elevated our minds to engage the Deity, to converse with the source and author of our beings, who gave us life and intelligence and perception and ability to receive and appreciate that which is divine.

We worship Thee today, our Father. We worship Thee here as many of our brethren worship Thee and many other churches of many denominations in various and diverse places in parts of the earth. We thank Thee, Father, that Thy people are not all here today. We thank Thee that they're not all in our group and not all affiliated with our denomination. Thou hast Thy people, O Lord, witnesses everywhere, among more people that love the name of Christ and that hold Him sacred and love Him and believe in Him and trust in Him. So we thank Thee we will join them today, Father.

We believe in the communion of saints. And we believe in the Church of the First Born and the General Assembly and all of those who love Thee and who are born of the Spirit and washed in the blood. Wilt Thou today grant, Our Father, that this service as it begins and as we go through, while we have eagerly in mind the thought of the days ahead with our missionary information, our missionary zeal, and our missionary giving? We pray that we may not divorce it for one moment from the love of Thee and the worship of Thee. We would not circle the earth to make one more convert and find, when we had made him, he was worse than he had been before, if they had only been converted to being an American instead of being a Christian.

We pray that Thou would grant to give us a New Testament vision and keep it before us, Lord, all the way through, everybody, everyone, all of us together, those who are here, those who will be coming and all the friends who will be gathering in from night to night and over the next week.

We pray Thee, our Father, for our country. We pray for our president and for those in his cabinet and for those who make our laws, for the governors of states and for all men in authority. We pray that Thou who didst speak and bend the will of Nebuchadnezzar and Darius, even when they didn't know it, Sovereign God, we pray that Thou would bend the Supreme Court and the Congress and the White House, and bend men to Thy purpose and will, even if they don't know it. If they're too busy even to think, bend them anyway. Answer the prayers of ten thousands of Thy people who've lived and died on this continent and have sent up holy prayers, tear-stained and washed in the blood of the Lamb. God, grant, we beseech Thee, that those prayers may not be lost and forgotten, but they may be remembered and answered for our land, for our country, this citadel of liberty and freedom. Help us not to abuse it, but to live as those who have been given a very wonderful gift and are reverently grateful to the One who gave it. Help us now through this service this morning, through the rest of the day and week through Jesus Christ our Lord, we pray.

Amen.

Ancient but True

Father, we thank Thee for these ancient words, ancient like the sun and modern like the sun. As old as the sun and the stars and older still, but yet as fresh and new and applicable as the latest thing that happened today. We thank Thee, Father, we thank Thee. We bless Thy name, that the Word depends upon the Word, that the written Word rests in the Living Word. And that the Living Word was before the world was, and through Him Thou didst speak the written Word, which we have, and so the link between the living Word and the written Word is a link of light.

These words encourage us today. And we will be encouraged in Thee, O God. We will hope in Thee. We will, we do, and we join to hope in Thee today and rejoice in Thee today. We bless Thy name, Father, and ask Thou Thy blessing to be upon us as we sing together, as we make our gifts which we also consecrate and believe to be a sacred act of worship. And as we expound the Word and as we talk together, O Lord, we believe that Thou wouldst speak through us and to us.

Help now today and bless this great city with all of its churches, big and little. Every mission and every place where the gospel is put forth, however simply, may the Truth abound. And we ask for our country, Lord, have mercy, we pray Thee, upon us, O God. Have mercy upon a country that's lost in its wealth, its money, its fun, its pleasure, its luxury. Save us, we pray, our God, from going the way of Greece and Rome, the way of Nineveh and Tyre. Save us, we pray, that our fires may not burn low on the hills and finally go out. Pity and spare us and remember our fathers who prayed and whose tears and sweat and blood stained and made sacred this continent.

God, bless Thou Thy people. And we pray for the country of the north of us, this friendly country where there are so many Christians. Bless Canada. Remember the work down in Mexico, we pray, just across the southern border, where men are giving out the Word and trying to reach people for centuries lost in pagan tradition. May many be illuminated with the gospel of Christ and saved. And O God, bless around the world in the mission stations of all denominations and all missionary societies. We pray for our own 825 or more, but we pray more, for greater numbers who belong to other societies.

God, bless and bring quickly, we pray, the Body into being so that Thou canst come and lead her as Thy bride on Thy arm into the Father's presence to be admired by all that know Thee. This we ask in the name of Jesus Christ our Lord.

Amen.

The Living Word

"The LORD reigneth, he is clothed with majesty; the LORD is clothed with strength, wherewith he hath girded himself: the world also is stablished, that it cannot be moved. Thy throne is established of old: thou art from everlasting. The floods have lifted up, O LORD, the floods have lifted up their voice; the floods lift up their waves. The LORD on high is mightier than the noise of many waters, yea, than the mighty waves of the sea. Thy testimonies are very sure: holiness becometh thine house, O LORD, forever." (Ps. 93:1–5)

Dear Heavenly Father, we bless Thee for the encouragement that we get by just reading together five verses out of the thousands inside Thy Word. Lord, Thou hast in Thy great kindness given us the Book and Thou hast breathed into it the breath of life, so that it is not a book filled with dead words, but a book that breathes and sees and hears, and we hear from Thee, the Living Word.

We pray now Thy blessing upon us this day. We thank Thee for this almost perfect day. And thank Thee for those who are present this morning. We pray for those who are away on various journeys. We pray Thou wouldst make this morning service one of complete fellowship in the blessed Holy Ghost. We pray, Lord, that we may hear Thee speak and that we may join hearts and minds around the table. We pray that we may meditate on

Thy Word. We pray that we may think on Thee and focus our attention upon Thee. We pray that we may love Thee and that we may learn to love Thee better today than we have up to now, that Thou would remove from our hearts the hindrances, whatever they may be. Let Thy grace be upon us, O God.

Remember Thy people. Thou knowest it's getting harder every month in some of our fields, dark fields of the world where Communism, Islam, or Catholicism or various forms of nationalism are squeezing in and shutting off the flow of truth, making it impossible for the people to carry on their witness freely.

We pray, O God, for Thy people. We pray, let Thy blessing be upon Thy church, Thy church all throughout the whole world. Be Thou in this great city of ours today. And let the anointing of the Spirit be upon every man who is bold and loving, to preach the Truth. We pray Thee for Okoboji in session today, and the numbers of our people that are there. We pray Thee for Beulah Beach, and for any others that may be in progress. We pray that great good may come of it all, separation and cleansing and deliverance and blessing. Help us today, we pray, through Jesus Christ. We ask it in His holy name.

Amen.

Quick, Powerful, and Sharp

Father, we thank Thee for Thy Word. It is our refuge, our hope, our stay, and assurance. It is everything to us. We love it, and have loved it, and wait to meditate on it in the night season, and rise to think about it in the morning. Bring it to our attention in every crisis and feast on it and pray that Thou wilt help us, that we may believe it and obey it. For in obedience to Thy Word, there comes good success and lo, Thou wilt be with us, as Thou wast with Moses.

Now Father, we're here to worship this Lord's Day morning. We thank Thee for this lovely day. We thank Thee for people. We thank Thee, Lord, for the sounds of life around us, the sounds that remind us that people are alive and living. Instead of death and destruction and smoking ruins, the sound of enemy bombers, there are human beings around us, living and populating the earth and working and building and planting, and growing old. O God, we pray, grant that we may not forget our testimony to those that are around about us.

Now, our Father, we asked for this home. For this man, who relatively young, has gone. God, bless those who remain to grieve, who've lost their father and lost one dear. We pray for them. We pray, that out of this, there might be, through Thy divine providence, some good yet, that the glory of Christ and the good of mankind may be served even in the death of this man.

We pray Thy blessing upon our people, Lord. Some of them traveling away and we ask for them. We pray Thee, give them wisdom and grace, and give a special dispensation of mercy to all of them. Bless Thy children. We think today, Lord, of how many of Thy children, truly Thy children, that are out on the highways. They're buzzing around over the continent. Maybe they shouldn't be, some of them, but they are. We pray for them all. We pray for them; they may be at lakes or anywhere else where there's danger—those that fly and those that drive. And we pray, Father, for those who may be around water and ask that Thou wilt shield and protect Thy people in a providential, miraculous way.

Now we trust Thee. Be with us this day. May Thy Word go forth, O God, and not return void. For Jesus' sake, who is our Lord.

Amen.

Hope-Filled Words

Father, we thank Thee, by the wonder of the Spirit's inworking. Thou dost take these words, drawn from an old, old book, written to a people that we are separated from by origin and by every human thing. And yet by Thy Spirit, they are applied to us as though they were written for us, and sent down just this morning. We bless Thee for these encouraging, hope-filled words. We thank Thee not only that Thou hast made them applicable to Israel and fulfilled them in Israel and will yet fulfill them, but we thank Thee for the thousands and multiplied thousands who have slept off, resting their heads upon such comforting words. We've gone into battle. We've gone to far parts of the earth. We've faced impossible situations, trusting in these words, and Thou dost never, never let them down. Thou didst bless them and keep them.

O Father, we pray through Jesus Christ our Lord that Thou wilt help us now. Since our fathers trusted Thee and were not forsaken, grant that we may trust Thee and we know we shall not be forsaken either. And we pray Thee, O God, Thou wilt be with our people scattered around over the earth. Be with the nation which we're a part, down on our human side. Bless our president, and we pray Thee for the Congress, soon to convene again. We pray Thee, O Lord God, for those who labor in these high places—simply men, poor men, men with breath in their nostrils. And oh, we ask Thee Father, to make them able for their jobs.

And we pray Thee for Thy work around the world in the cause of missions wherever there are men and women preaching the gospel. We pray Thou would bless every radio program. Thou would bless every effort of men and women to get a language, to learn it, to preach in it, and to win people, and teach them, and instruct them in the way they should go and baptize them, and make them into little groups and form churches. Help Thou, we pray Thee our God, this day. Give us a cheerful outlook on life and let us expect that we shall see a performance of all things promised us. Bless the sick, and the bereaved, and the troubled, and the distressed. We ask it in the name of Jesus Christ our Lord.

Amen.

4

AUTHENTICITY

"So shall the king greatly desire thy beauty: for he is thy Lord; and worship thou him" (Ps. 45:11). Here's the truth upon which we build. Simply this, that God made everything for a purpose. And the purpose in making man was to have somebody capable, properly and sufficiently, to worship Him, to satisfy His own heart. But that man fell by sin and now is failing to carry out the creative purpose. He is like a cloud without water and gives no rain. Like a sun that gives no heat, or a star that gives no light, or a tree that no longer gives any fruit, or a bird that no longer sings, or a harp that is silent and no longer gives off music.

"He is Thy Lord, worship Thou Him." Here is something that we want to settle, and that is that God wants us to worship

Him. The devil would like to tell us, or our own unbelieving minds, that God does not particularly want us to worship Him. Yes, we think we owe it to Him, but God isn't concerned. The truth is, God wants us to worship Him. We're not unwanted children. God wants us to worship Him, I repeat. Why else would it be when Adam had sinned and broken his fellowship, and the harp of Adam had become unstrung and the voice of Adam had died in his throat. Why was it that when God came in the cool of the day to talk with Adam, he couldn't find him and cried, "Adam, where art thou?" It was God seeking worship from an Adam that had sinned.

God finds something in us. It is something that He put there, but it's there. My friend, unbelief is of several kinds or rather, there are several phases or facets to unbelief. One of them is this, that we don't think we're as bad as God says we are, that's one. And if we don't have faith in God's Word concerning our badness, we'll never repent. Then, there is another facet of faith. It is this, that we don't believe that we are as dear to God as He says we are. And we don't believe that we're as precious and that He desires us as much as He says He does.

If we could suddenly have a baptism of pure cheerful belief that God wanted me and that God wanted me to worship Him and that God wanted me to pray and admire Him and praise Him, it could transform this Christian fellowship and change us overnight into the most radiantly happy people on the North American continent!

"So shall the King greatly desire thy beauty, and He is thy Lord so worship thou Him."

Clean Dwellings

O dear Lord, time is short and the hour is late and we have such little time to go. And religion has gotten organized now, Thy religion Lord Jesus, so that anybody can do it, anybody. We don't have to have the gifts anymore. The tragedy and the terror of it all! But Lord, still men build their Babylons, call them by Thy name, but they go down and perish.

Oh, we want our work to last. For soon we shall be where the wicked cease from troubling, and there the weary be at rest, and only what the Holy Ghost does will last. We would yield our earthly vessels. We would bring our empty vessels. We would, if need be, come and ask Thee to begin to scrub the rust and the filth until our hearts are shiny, clean repositories for the blessed Spirit.

God bless everybody that listens tonight. Now, make us all see this. Make us all understand it, Lord. How tragic it is to peter out at last and be cobblers in the Kingdom of God, and fool around and put patches on the roof and prop up the temple with sticks. O God, and it's everywhere men are doing it. We confess, Lord God, that we feel like being sick when we read the pages of the Sunday papers and some of those religious magazines. Adam's brain is busy trying to do God's work. We wonder, Lord, if it isn't offering strange fire on the altar of God. We wonder if it won't bring judgment in that Day. O Lord, save us from offering strange fire. Any fire we offer we want to be of the altar, Thy fire.

Bless us now as we separate. Please don't let us eke our way through where we are tonight and forget all about this. Great God, we pray Thee, give us gravity. And the boy in his early teens is here tonight with exuberance and nervous energy, make him grave and serious. And we think of Thy sixteen-year-old handmaid who yielded herself to the Holy Ghost and was the instrument in some places of the revival. We don't excuse our sixteen-year-olds who think they're cooped in the pasture field. We don't excuse the parents who think that their children ought to be permitted to just play, when actually Lord God, the crisis is, the world's on fire. And the judgment is drawing near and the coming of the Lord draweth nigh.

My God, wilt Thou send us out, grave and thoughtful, to meditate on Thy Word? Give us, we pray Thee, desire and determination, and then push us on until we're pushed over the cliff in desperation. And then, as a mother eagle stirs up her nest and then dives down and catches her young, wilt Thou catch us and fill us and gift us? And the work we do, though it may not be vast, will have eternity in its heart.

Amen.

First Century Church

Our Father, we see Thee before we see troubles or difficulties. And we see Thee holding the world in Thy hand and taking up the isles as a very little thing, and counting all the nations of the earth as dust grains in the balance. Thou art the great God. We thank Thee. Thou art bigger than man's woes and greater than his troubles. Where man's sins abounded, Thy grace did much more abound, and where our troubles multiplied, Thy deliverance was more multiplied.

So Father, Thou seest the conditions we note this morning, as churches all over the city and perhaps most of the country are noting now absenteeism resulting from a wave of Asian flu. And now we pray Thee, Lord, that Thou would put Thy hand of life upon everybody. And let not death take any toll, but let there be only life. Help us and give us courage and patience to endure the inconvenience of it while it passes across. But oh, we pray Thee, that where the blood is on the doorpost, there the angel may pass over, and that we may there be protected by Thy mighty grace.

And Father, we pray that Thou wilt today help us as we gather as an assembly of Thy people. Father, grant, we pray, the sense of gathering, the sense of being an assembly of people gathered in from the north and south and east and west, to the person of the Savior, ministering to the Lord, gathered around the person of Jesus.

O God, this is our earnest yearning today, that instead of it being a church service in the modern sense of the word, it might be a New Testament gathering of Christians who have taken Jesus to be all in all and are resting upon Him, and believe that He died and rose and lives and pleads and is coming again. In the meantime, He is in His people and the Kingdom of God is within us, and Thy presence is really here—more really, truly here than anything we can see or touch.

We pray for the sick. We pray for the bereaved. We ask Thee for this family and ask Thee, Father, that Thy mercy may be over them. And we pray Thee, for those who are sick with one kind or another disease. We pray Thee, O Thou Shepherd of Israel and Thou Physician, wilt Thou stretch out Thine hand and heal and graciously, graciously, bless?

Now, we pray for Thy church all over the world. We pray for our country. We pray for Thy work and the cause of evangelism and missions wherever men are found. And may we this day, this hour, this time, right now, have faith that finds Thee and sees Thee and gathers Thee to ourselves. We ask it in Christ's name.

Amen.

An Accurate Name

Our Heavenly Father, we ask Thee, please God, grant that we might live in character with our profession. That holy, worthy name, whereby we are called. We have called Thee Abba Father. We have stayed our heart on Thee. And others have looked at us and said, "There's a man of God. There's a woman of God. There's a mother in Israel. There's a young Dorcas. There's a Hannah." O Father, look us through and through and if Thou dost find anything out of character with such names, remove them quickly, Lord, by the blood of Jesus and the fire of the Spirit, that we may be what we profess to be. This we ask in the name of Jesus Christ.

Amen.

Power, Fellowship, and Conformity

O Lord Jesus, Lord Jesus, Thou knowest we live in a world where perils and dangers are on every hand. And life is short and time is fleeting and judgment is coming. And Satan is busy and all the fiends are squaring themselves across the path trying to prevent us from going ahead. But we hear Thee calling from the mountain peak. We want to know Thee in the power of Thy resurrection and the fellowship of Thy suffering and be made conformable unto Thy death. We want to know the beauty and wonder that is Thee.

We pray for these who've requested prayer, O Christ Jesus, Christ Jesus. Christ Jesus, Thou who didst come in olden times in the form of a dove and sat upon each of them as fire. And Thou who didst come to Peter and to the Moravians and to the saints of New England. Thou who didst come, O Lord, in spots here and there in Borneo and Korea. Oh, withhold not Thy glory from us. We cry, show us Thy glory, Lord, show us Thy glory, and teach us how to go on.

And now, grant, we pray, that this may be a good week and if the devil makes it the worst week we've ever had, we'll understand it. We'll have a naked intent and determination, and will calmly, quietly believe—even though we should be attacked. Even though the darkness should settle over us, we'll know it's the cloud of unknowing. It's the dark night of the soul that precedes the bright morning of the heart. And we won't be frightened. We know Thou didst go through the Garden and through the cross and into the darkness and out of the darkness and into the tomb and out of the tomb and into the glory.

So, wilt Thou lead these, lead us, and lead this church? And oh, we pray, bring us to a place where soon we may be under grace, spiritually prepared for a mighty outpouring of the Holy Ghost. An outpouring that shall bring, in reality, that which everybody's talking about and nobody has, and we shall come back to New Testament spirituality, back to Book of Acts Christianity again. Then maybe out from us here there shall flow streams into the desert way, and fire that shall touch churches and groups everywhere. Bless us as we wait. And above all things, show us Thyself, Thyself, Lord, and show us Thy glory. Hide us in the rock as Thou passest by and show us Thy glory, so that all the glory of this world shall appear as ashes after that wonderous sight. This we ask in the holy name of Jesus.

Amen.

True Belief

O Lamb of God, I love Thee so, I would with Thee life's journeys go. And O Lord Jesus, we would resist the world and spurn the flesh, and put our pride on the cross and die with Thee, that we might live with Thee.

O Lord Jesus, we pray for these who've heard. Some of them we don't know. Some of them we do. Some of them we believe are real Christians, some on the way. But O God, Thou knowest every one of us deeply, deeply. We want to be ready. We want to be ready, Lord, when Thou comest.

We pray, help us, that we might be willing to inconvenience ourselves, to upset our neat plans, to stir up our fur-lined nest and to carry a cross; and to go where we're sent; to give up what's wrong and begin what's right, and cease to do evil and learn to do good.

O Lord, the church has been betrayed by easy-believism.

And we've been told "just believe and you're all right." And that's true, but not true as they teach it. So help us to believe truly, Lord, believe in faith. Believe, with a cross on our shoulder. Believe, but believe with our back to the world, believe with our faces toward the Light, and believe with a sword and a hammer in our hands. Believe, Lord God, doing something.

Bless Thou this congregation. Help them, we pray, each and every one, not to lose what they've heard tonight in song and sermon, but to go home and think it over, pray about it, and earnestly seek to be in that number. We sing, "I want to be in that number." But Lord, we don't mean it. We smile, laugh and giggle and go on. We really want to mean it, Lord. We want to be in that number when the saints come marching in. Bless us now as we bring our service to a close. In Christ's name.

Amen.

Something Fresh

O God our Father, our Father who art in heaven. We lift our voices to Thee in this day of trouble and distress. This day when our leaders are scared. This day when men of great genius tremble, and with hushed voice testify before great committees of Congress, the peril of the nation. This day, O God, when there's been a revival of Catholicism, Buddhism, Islam,

Shintoism, and Taoism. This day when Spiritism, Jehovah's Witnesses, and all the cults are growing like a fire in dry grass. O God, how we need help in this hour.

We need help, Lord, we need help. We don't just want more of what we have, we want something fresh and new that we don't have. We don't just want more numbers. We want a new type of Christian. We want a new breed. We want a people, O God, who are anointed, and who have the very nature of Christ, who follow the Lamb, who believe the Bible, who are disciples and know the Lordship of Christ. Here one, and here one there, two here, ten there, scattered in groups—heartsick and willful. They're trying to find again the holy way. Great God, lead us into that way.

Here in this church, lead us in, Lord. Lead in our board. Lead in our people so that we may show the way to others, Lord. Thank Thee for those who are ready to listen, even if they don't obey yet. But may we begin to obey soon, and by obedience steel up our faith. Now, Lord Jesus, send us out from here, reverent and serious minded. Help us not to joke away what we've heard and put ourselves in a mental state where we lose everything we have before we get to the door. Graciously meet us and bless us. We ask it in Jesus Christ's precious name.

Amen.

New Glory

Gracious Lord Jesus, save anyone who isn't saved and restore anybody who might have wandered a bit from the holy highway. Give us these Sunday nights before us, give us, we plead, O God, such a time of New Testament Christianity, such a time of Book of Acts glory, as has not been known ever in this church before.

Bring the people in who ought to hear this. We know the rank and the file. We know the lovers of this world. We know those who want this world and the next, who want to carry a cross and have their fun. We know they won't get anything out of it, but there are enough people, Lord, that will. Send them.

Now wilt Thou, we pray Thee, bless the young people, as a little later they go to have their hymn sing? May their testimonies and songs be inspired by the Holy Ghost. Bless, we beseech Thee, O God, all the people. We want to ask one more time, asking it together, that Thou wilt save all Christians on the highways—all Christians from all churches that are truly Christians—don't let them be among the casualties who die on the highway. All this we ask in Jesus' holy name.

Amen.

Satisfied Christians

Dear Lord Jesus, our Redeemer, our Advocate above, who for our salvation did shed Thy most precious blood. We appeal to Thee tonight, O Christ, faith is thinning out and becoming bloodless. O Christ, raise up a people who will be New Testament Christians, who will be satisfied with worship and good deeds and witness and holy living, that they might know noble dying and a holy hereafter.

For Jesus' sake, we pray Thee, for all who listen to gospel preaching tonight, this rainy night, this night of storms. Bless Thou the people who will be driving, the people out on the roads, people out on the streets, people where the shiny streets make lights multiply and sometimes it's dangerous. Bless all those who have driven to church and will be driving home, will walk to church and will be walking home, who've taken some public means of transportation, that will be taking it back.

Gracious heavenly Father, bless Thy sheep. Bless every man of God who about this time will be giving, or a little later, his invitation. Let there be those who will be saved this night. Let there be those who will determine they will follow the Lamb, that no matter what the circumstances, they will turn their back on the world and they will believe and will follow. Grant it, for Christ's sake. We ask this in Jesus Christ's holy name.

Amen.

Precious Treasure

We thank Thee. We thank Thee for all of Thy people everywhere, of every denomination, who believe Thy Word and trust Thy Son and love Thee and call Thee Father, which art in heaven. We thank Thee, Father. We thank Thee that Thou hast a people of every color and nationality and race and tongue and people. And they shall stand with the Lamb and shall rejoice together and sing, "Worthy is the Lamb that was slain to receive honor and glory and power."

We pray now Thou wilt help us that we might be worthy members of such a glorious body. Help us, we pray, to bow or to lift our hats, to genuflect every time we think of Thy people, Thy church—Thy people, Lord, from whom Thou didst cast Thine eye in invitation, who heard Thee and came. We see them moving about, and we see them die. And we see them ill, and we look at the worst part of it, the physical, human side of them. But within, there is a deposit, the treasure. Thou hast given them Thy very nature and they're Thine, and they're infinitely more precious than all outer space and all the galaxies that make up the Milky Way, and all the angels in heaven and all the seraphim. For they are the apple of Thine eye. We thank Thee for them and ask Thy blessing upon them today. All Thy church, the household of God, in heaven and in earth, triumphant and militant, gone and those who are still here, worshiping, praying, resisting temptation, and working, and laboring and waiting.

Now, we trust Thee for the whole country, for our president and for those in authority, and for all for whom we should pray this morning. Make this a good and Christ-honoring service. In His holy name, we ask it.

Amen.

Power and Authority

Our Heavenly Father, Jesus Christ our Lord, we pray that Thou wilt help us. It's easy to preach it, Lord, but the flesh is weak and the world's magnetic attraction is very strong, but these two together, along with the devil, are weak compared with the Holy Ghost whom Thou hast given to the church. "All power is given unto Me." That's authority. "Ye shall receive power when the Holy Ghost comes on you." That's power. Now we have these both. We pray Thee, help us that we may go forth to exercise authority, and to have power. That this, which is impossible to the flesh, may become not only possible but completely and entirely true in our lives.

Graciously bless us and meet us in our varying services, long or short, here or there, wherever they may be. Grant, we pray, that beginning now we may cease to trust in the pluses of Christianity, even however precious they may be and how comforting, and make Thee our sanctuary, and sanctify Thee and set Thee aside as our all in all, and dwell in Thy heart. Grant this, we pray.

Let these people go on to victory, to success in the troublesome and irksome weeks that lie just ahead of them. Holy Father, through Jesus Christ, grant that this plant which was planted by the Spirit may not perish, but may grow, and surprise, and confound the devil, and that it may have branches over the wall, and yet bear fruit and fulfill all the truth that says that I will be better unto you than in times past. That the tomorrow of this fellowship may be infinitely beyond the yesterdays of the fellowship, through Jesus Christ our Lord.

Amen.

BACKSLIDING

When we pray, we can approach God with confidence, for our faith rests upon His character, not upon promises. Promises are as good as the character of the one who made the promise. So when I read my Bible, I have a promise. This is the confidence we have in Him. If you ask anything according to His will, He hears us. And if He hears us, we have the petition as a promise from God.

Jesus said, "Whatsoever ye shall ask in my name, I will give it" (John 16:23). There's a promise from God. How good is the promise? It's as good as the One who made it. How good is that? Faith says God is God, the Holy God who cannot lie. The God who is infinitely rich and can make good on all of His promises. The God who is infinitely honest and never cheated anybody.

The God who is infinitely true and never told any lies. That's how good a promise is that God makes. It's as good as God is, because God made it. This is the confidence that we have in Him, to glorify God by faith. There's God, not just the promises.

In the Bible, we learn what God wants to do for us, we learn what to ask for. We learn what God has willed to us. We learn what we may claim as our heritage. We learn from the promises how we should pray. But faith always rests down upon the character of God. He made heaven and earth and holds the world in His hand and measures the dust of the earth in a balance and the sky He spreads out like a mantel. Remember, the Great God Almighty is not your servant. You're His servant. He is your Father. You are His child. He sits in heaven. You're on earth. Angels veil their faces before the God who cannot lie.

I think it would be a wonderful thing that every preacher in America would for one solid year preach about God: who He is, His attributes, His perfection, His being; what kind of God He is, why we dare to trust Him, why we can trust Him, why we should trust Him, why we can love Him, why we should love Him, why we would dare not fall short of loving Him. Keep on preaching God—God, the Triune God—and keep on until He fills the whole horizon and the whole world! Faith would spring up like grass for the watercourse. And let a man get up and preach a promise, and the whole congregation would say, "I can trust that one. Look who made it. Look who made it!"

Confidence may be slow in coming, but you can have confidence in God as you go to Him in the merits of His Son and ask Him and claim His promises. God will lead you. God will help you in your need, whatever it may be.

Delivery from Indifference

O Lord Jesus, we profess to be a company of believers. We profess that we believe in Thee. And we feel a cool breath over us tonight, Lord. We feel not the hot breath of the devil, but the cold breath of indifference. And we would pray against it. We would lift up our voices to Thee, the Christ of God, and ask Thee to breathe on us with Thy warm breath.

We pray Thou deliver us, O God, from indifference, laziness, carelessness, lack of desire, and all of these little foxes that spoil the vine. O Lord, we pray, we pray today that Thou wouldst move in upon us as the Shekinah of old moved in on Israel. And Lord, if You did it, it had to be unknown to us. Up to now, we haven't seen, nor felt, nor heard.

O Christ, Thou art risen from the dead. Thou hast appeared unto Peter and five hundred brethren at once, and to Paul, as one born out of due time, and Thou art seated at the right hand of the Majesty in the heavens. From Thy vantage point of power, O Christ, help us tonight. Help us, Lord, for tomorrow we die. Help us, Lord. And help us as we try to hear the Word of God. Speak, Lord, for Thy servants listen. Speak, Lord, through Thy Word as in ancient days. Open heaven and let Thy glory shine upon us and give us, we beseech Thee, visions of the King, high and lifted up with His train filling the temple.

Oh God, save us from this dull routine. Save us, we pray

Thee, from this circular grave, where we march around and round and round. O God, do something new. Thou hast said, "Ye have camped long enough in this mount. Get thee up into the land that I will show thee." Help us tonight, Lord, even tonight. Some of us here might move forward and get up and move. If we have not large numbers, Lord, those who are here can do it. Thou didst preach Thy greatest sermons to a half dozen or a dozen men. We pray that Thou, Lord, will do things that'll be significant and epochal, and be a turning point in somebody's life tonight, by the blood of the everlasting covenant and by the power of the cross where You died.

O Lord Jesus, we pray that Thou wilt fumigate, and drive out, and cure, and kill all the anti-holy, anti-good, anti-God, devilish germs that infest and infect the hearts of people in this terrible generation. Help now, Lord, and fulfill the Word that "you shall receive power when the Holy Ghost is come upon you." May we hear from Thee tonight. We ask it in Jesus' name. Amen.

Understand and See

O Lord, Thou who didst patiently deal with Thy servant Nicodemus, here with us tonight. Thou knowest, Lord, that the flesh with all of its pressure, and the world with its distractions, and the devil with his wiles, unite to make our hearts fat and our ears dull of hearing and our eyes blind.

Oh, come, Lord Jesus. Do for us what Thou didst do for the disciples when Thou didst open their understanding and enable them to see. O Lord, we pray, give us sharp eyes, willing feet, quick hands, and above all, humble hearts as we think together over this truth discussed so long ago, living still without any diminution of content or quality, remaining everlastingly the same as Thou who didst give it. Help us now as we wait in Thy presence. For Christ's sake.

Amen.

Worldly Dangers

Father, O God, Thou art near us. Thou art here. Like Jacob, we're tempted to say, Thou art in this place and I knew it not. But we did know it after a fashion. This is none other than the gate of heaven. This is the house of God, Bethel. We will raise our altar here at this Presence.

Now, we pray for men and women, and particularly young people, who are charmed. The serpent of the world is charming them like a bird, and they gaze with fascination upon all the showy glamour of the world. They would die to become famous. Women here would give twenty years off their lives for five years to be a movie star.

Great God, we're sick, sick, sick inside, that we have sought the gutter instead of the clouds. We have learned to love and live in the mire and imitate and follow the filthiest, lowest, most profane element in society. And there is a Light, and men don't see it, and a Voice and they don't hear it, and a Presence and they don't feel it. Oh, we pray, get hold of men and women and young people and children tonight, and pull them out of this mud, moral and intellectual mud. Get them out of it, we pray Thee.

We pray that Thou will give to all of us who've been here tonight a renewed and vivid sense of the sacredness and spirituality of the world that Thou hast created. Sin we have no track with. There's nothing good that can be said about it. No eloquence can remove from it the ugly bestiality of sin. But apart from sin, O God, Thou art in the world. Thou art here.

We pray Thee, help us morning and night and all during day and night and wherever we may be, to keep in contact with Thee, knowing that He is in the world. And the great grief of the world is, the world knows enough. But oh, we Christians can say, thank Thee, Father, we know Thee. We know Thee through Jesus Christ Thy Son. We call Thee Father. We have called Thee Abba Father. We have stayed our hearts on Thee. Blessed be Thy Name.

Now we trust Thee through Jesus Christ our Lord.

Amen.

Hear, Understand, and Obey

Father, we who are gathered here are by that very fact shown to be well off and prosperous and healthy enough to be out. Therefore, Lord God, we bring only thanksgiving to Thee. For those who cannot be here, but would, we pray for them. For those who could be here and are, we give Thee thanks, and ask for a restoration to help for those who are absent because of illness. And any who may be absent because of indifference, they're in greater need of healing than if they were flat on their back with some dread disease. So wilt Thou, we pray thee, heal the hearts of the indifferent and the bodies of the sick, and the minds of the weary?

And God, we pray in Christ's name, help us that this day, this day of rest and gladness, this first day of the week, may be a good day. And may we know what to do with it and how to use it. May we know, Lord, how to improve the shining hours, not let them go by as golden caskets filled with jewels of the mind—and having once passed us, never to be recalled again. We pray Thee, help us to be wise and to so number our days that we may know how to apply our hearts unto wisdom.

We pray Thee for the friends who are out from this church to the various parts of the world. Lord, bless them. We think of the missionaries and we think also of the many preachers and teachers that are out from here. They're all scattered over the world and are standing to preach the Word or teach the Word or to give the gospel message for the first time. Wilt Thou bless them this day, O Lord, and open ears and eyes and pierce, we pray Thee, the stuffed-up ears of the listeners, that they may hear the very voice of the Holy Spirit?

Father, without Thy help we can do nothing; we know that. We can't even want to do right without Thy Spirit. Oh, then Lord, Thy Spirit give in great measure. Be Thou prevenient. Be Thou there first. Be Thou within us, we pray, to desire, that it may kindle ours. Be Thou there to love, that our love may take fire. Be Thou there in us in faith, that our faith may come up like a flame. Lord, be Thou with us sending all that ought to come by way of finances, to prosper the work at home and abroad and make the Word, we pray, to be rich and true and good. And may we worship Thee in song. Give us a good afternoon. Bring us up to a wonderful meeting tonight. This we ask through Jesus Christ our Lord.

Amen.

Forgive and Cleanse

We can say with the hymnist, shame on us, that we've left Thee standing there. Shame on us! We repent before Thee. We're sorry for ourselves, for our friends. We're sorry, Lord, for our neighbors, our fellow Americans. Sorry, O Lord.

We grieve and repent before Thee. Millions attend ballgames, and millions attend prizefights and millions attend shows. And they count their wealth in millions and multiplied millions and they buy what they will, where they will. Because men spend their dollars, Thy dollars, freely for lusts and pleasures and entertainment and possessions.

O Lord Jesus, the poor, little, unpainted churches, the poor half-paid preachers, the poor, groaning, old organs and badly tuned pianos, and cheaply constructed buildings, all tell the same thing. But not very many have received what they need. We're ashamed tonight, Lord. We're ashamed, Lord Jesus. The crowds are not in church tonight. They're in theaters, skating rinks, dance halls, body houses, gambling dens. But they're not in churches. We thank Thee for everyone that is, but they're not many.

Oh, we're ashamed, Lord. We're ashamed for our friends. Ashamed, Lord, that they have rejected Thee so successfully, so long. They're guests in Thy house, boarders sitting at Thy table, breathing Thy air and drinking Thy water, sleeping on Thy sweet earth, eating Thy fruits. But they rejected Thee.

O Lord Jesus, we're ashamed and we repent and we're sorry. Forgive, O Lord, we pray Thee. Forgive us. Forgive, O Lord, the half-saved Christians. Forgive the lazy half-backslidden Christian. Hot, spiritual preaching only drives them underground. They sneak underground and go and do it anyway. Keep it from pastor and keep it from the teachers, but do it anyway. O God, how ashamed we are of all this. Holy Ghost, we grieve Thee, and a lot of us tremble in the corner. We've given Thee no place. We're sorry.

O Thou Dove, Thou dost flutter over us and can't find a place for the sole of your foot. We're ashamed. Oh, make this church a clean place for the sole of Thy foot to light upon, blessed Thou of God. Come flutter down upon us with Thy light and strength and power and grace and healing and joy and loveliness. Come and flutter down on us. Forgive, we pray Thee, the pig sties of our hearts. May we cleanse them and dump them out and fix up the temple and say, "Come in, Lord Jesus." O Shekinah of God, we pray Thee, come to the temples of our hearts.

Lord, we pray for these five persons who have raised their hands and asked us to remember them. O Lord Jesus, the world is so full of temptations and the magnetism of the world is all but impossible to resist. But these people want to do it. They want to turn from everything that grieves the Lord and follow Him. They want to be Thine completely, fully. And we pray for them. Thou said "pray one for another."

We lift our hearts in prayer now and ask, O Lord, that you will help these five people to put away their resistance, throw down all opposition and neatly surrender now their hearts to Thee. For Thee to come in, take over, set up Thy throne and reign from within, King of their lives, by grace. We pray Thee, Lord Jesus, even right now. Help these friends tonight, for Jesus' sake.

Amen.

Dissatisfied Deliverance

O Lord Jesus, Thou knowest the propensity of the human heart to backslide. Thou knowest how quickly the temperature of the human spirit cools off. Thou knowest how easy it is to become satisfied with ourselves, to be at ease in Zion, to invent instruments of music and stretch ourselves on beds of ivory, and drink wine out of bowls, and care nothing for the captivity of Israel. Lord, we see this among us.

Oh, deliver us, we pray Thee, from complacency. Deliver us from fallow ground. Deliver us from the unplowed heart. Deliver us from deadly contentment. We beseech Thee, deliver us from taking by faith and not receiving. Forgive us, we pray Thee, for our conventional Christianity. Forgive us, we pray Thee, because we're afraid to be extreme. O Lord, cleanse our hearts from cowardice. And deliver us, we beseech Thee, from being little, frightened creatures in the hour when we need lions and prophets and bold reformers and seers who wear the crown of spiritual ascendancy and rule by prayer in the spoken Word.

We beseech Thee, disturb us. Upset us. Let us not settle

down to the grind of business, but rather let us, we pray Thee, while we do the business, always have the subconscious yearning, the longing, even if we have to push it out of our mind a little, may it come flaring back, like a fire, to burn in our bones, until we seek Thy face and are filled with the Holy Ghost. We ask it in Christ's name.

Amen.

Cooling Hearts

O Lord Jesus, look on us with Thy love, Thy undying affection—Thy love, that a few hours later would die for a cursing apostle. That love hasn't lost any of its content. No weaker, no smaller, but it is as big as God is big and as eternal as God is eternal.

O Lord Jesus, we're Thy sheep, professed sheep. And the world is big and the devil is going about like a roaring lion. The temptations are strong and the flesh is weak, and maybe some of us are cooling off inside our hearts. Please, Lord Jesus, look at us before it's too late. Help us to get enough of it quick, before it's too late. Please, Lord, don't let it harden into permanent backsliders, people who have lost their conscience and can no longer grieve because they can't grieve. No longer sorrow, because they don't feel sorrow.

Oh, we plead, Lord, look at us again today in our hearts.

We're no better than Peter. But maybe, Lord, there may be some who, like Peter, have sneaked out of discipleship, or least inwardly they have. Oh, look on us, Lord, and break our hearts. Look on us and make us weep. Give the grace of tears this morning, Lord, O Jesus, a few tears. If we knew that we could have this morning ten thousand dollars laid in our offering plates for the church and for missions, we'd be glad. But if we knew instead we were to have ten thousand tears of grief and repentance and penitence and faith and hope and joy, we would lay the ten thousand dollars away and take the tears that we might weep, because we can't weep. Oh, help us this morning, in Jesus' name.

Amen.

Return to First Love

O God, Thou seest the infiltrating enemy, the world, and the flesh, and the devil. They infiltrate, they brainwash, they persuade, they discourage, they try to intimidate. Oh, but make us Thy children to live in the midst of it, as gold in the midst of a fire, and not be destroyed; but only to become ductile and fluid, and able to be shaped into whatever form Thou dost, in Thy great artistry, choose for us.

Bless now, we pray Thee, everybody this morning here. We would be honest with ourselves, but we also would throw ourselves out upon Thy love and know that we're heard because of our Friend above in honor of His dying love. Grant us, we beseech Thee, walk out of here with the determination that, come what may, lose what we may by way of money or friends, we're going to return to our first love and seek to love Thee and to walk with Thee and to walk in Thy holy presence with lives so pure and so good that there can be no honest criticism made against us by our enemies, that's everyone.

We pray Thee, restore the weakest and bring back the one who's gone the farthest. Lift us all up and encourage us, through Jesus Christ our Lord.

Amen.

Sight Restoration

O God our Father, God our Father, Thou knowest how easy it is to backslide and not know it. Thou knowest how easy it is to have a name to live, and be dead. Thou knowest how easy it is to become part of a troupe of jolly church people, chattering and giggling our way along while the world grows old and the judgment draws near, and Hell enlarges her borders, and the Antichrist prepares himself to take over while the world is unifying itself and getting ready for a head, a president, a king.

O God, and Thy church playing and fooling and saying "I

am rich and increased with goods and have need of nothing." We have more people attending. We have more money than we ever had and our churches cost more. Our schools are full and our programs are many, forgetting, O my God, that the quality of our Christianity has been greatly impaired.

Oh, restore again, we cry, restore again to Thy church her vision of Thee. Restore again to Thy church her sight of the Great God. Show us Thy face, Thy lovely face, a permanent view of majesty. We will not say a transient gleam, O my God—these transient gleams are too many. We want a permanent sight of Thee in all Thy wonder!

O God, men sin on and on and on, and they treat religion, smile at it and laugh about it and tolerate it. But, O God, we've lost our fear and our majesty and our awe. Give back to us, we pray Thee, Majesty in the heavens. Give back to us the sight of Majesty again, that we can know how wonderful Thou art, and Thy Majesty how bright, and how beautiful Thy mercy seat in depths of burning light.

Send us to our homes to pray and to walk about, knowing that we're in the Garden indeed, even as Thou didst walk in the Garden in the cool of the day and Adam hid. Oh, how many of us, Lord, hide behind one thing or another because we are not morally and spiritually prepared to come out and walk with Thee. But Enoch walked with Thee and was not, because God took him. And Moses looked upon Thy face, and his face, it came to pass, did shine. O God, send us out not only to make converts, but send us out, we pray Thee, to glorify the Father and to hold up the beauty of Jesus Christ to men. All this we ask in the name of Jesus Christ our Lord, and all the people said amen.

Amen.

6

SURRENDER

WHEN THE LORD JESUS was asked what is the greatest commandment of the Law, He said, "This is the greatest commandment: Thou shalt love the Lord thy God with all thy heart and with all thy mind and strength, with all the power in you, you are to love God" (Matt. 22:37).

Adoration is love with fear and wonder and yearning and awe. When Jesus walked among men, He affected them two ways, and sometimes, two ways at once. He affected them with a magnetic drawing and He affected them with a fear that repulsed.

The same heart that yearned for God with a great yearning, also in awesome fear, might have been repulsed by the greatness and elevation and magnitude of the Being we call God. This is not only to love, but it's to feel a possessiveness, a crying mind. Go through your Bible and see how many times that men say "mine" to God, "mine, mine" to God. They tell us the personal pronoun shouldn't be used in religion. That's the difficulty with us when we're using it about ourselves and about what we've done and about where we've been and about who we know and about what we own. But we're afraid to use it about our relation to God.

The great reformer Martin Luther once said the whole heart of religion lies in its personal pronoun. When the human heart cries with a psalmist or a prophet or an apostle or a mystic and says, "mine, mine mine, God is mine" and when the human heart worships God and says, "mine," God says, "Yes, I am. I'm yours. So shall the king greatly desire thy beauty. For He is thy Lord, worship thou Him" (Ps. 45:11). And at times, all this rises to the place of breathless silence, wrapped in deep adoring silence. Jesus, Lord, I dare not move, lest I lose the smallest saying to catch the ear of love.

Now when all these are present—these mental, emotional, and spiritual factors—they're present in varying degrees. But when they're present, they're present in song and in praise and in prayer and in mental prayer, in inward prayer and in ejaculatory prayer, kept blazing by long seasons of prayer. They condition our thoughts and our words and our deeds. They give us a philosophy of life. They give us an outlook, a vantage point. They give us what the moderns like to call a scale of values. That's all right. Just because the liberals use it, don't throw it away. But they give us a scale of values.

We value some things more than others and we learn what is valuable and what isn't. And it hallows every place and every time and every task. It can do that for all of us. And it gives back the glory which Jesus had with the Father before the world was. It prepares the heart to worship.

Yielded Hearts

We thank Thee, O High Priest who has sat down on the right hand of the throne of the Majesty in the heavens and who carries our names on Thy shoulders and in Thy hands and on Thy breast, carrying us and supporting us before the presence of the eternal Majesty.

We worship Thee this day. We thank Thee, O High Priest, victorious, triumphant, vindicated by the right hand of God, the Father Almighty, from the accusations of Thy foes, though put to death in the flesh. Thou was raised in the Spirit and now glorified. Thou art our High Priest forever, our Savior by the throne of grace. We would worship Thee in the midst of this day, in this dark world full of hostilities and threats and dangers and walking deaths on every side.

We hide ourselves in Thy wounds, O High Priest, slain for us. We have nothing to offer but our hearts. We have no gift that would please Thee. Though we were to offer Thee golden crowns, Thou would smile, for the streets of the city are paved with gold. We would offer Thee jewels. It would mean nothing to Thee, for the very gates and walls are studded with jewels.

But, Lord, we offer Thee our hearts and this, we thank Thee, is unique in nature and in all creation. Nothing like it can be found. Redeemed moral beings with wills of their own, offering Thee their voluntary devotion and worship. This, O Lord, we thank Thee, Thou dost receive. Take it, Lord, we pray by the blood of the everlasting covenant, and make it real and wonderful to us as it is to Thee, the worship of our hearts.

Wilt Thou bless this morning service? Give us an unusual sense of Thy presence. We're conscious of the absence of some. But Lord, we pray, more than make up for the absence of some by Thy conscious presence. For Thou being present would mean more than if a thousand of the best Christians in the world were suddenly to appear. Thy presence would outshine all that, dear and wonderful as that might be.

Now, bless Thou Thy people throughout the earth. Help, we pray Thee, in poor Asia. Poor, distraught and bleeding and fleeing in grave danger and in whole sections of the world, soon closed to the gospel unless Thou dost speak the word that will roll the seas away. O Lord, remember that Thou art the Lord God of Moses, and the Lord God of Elijah, and of Elisha. Let us see in the mountains chariots and horsemen prepared to defend Israel against the foe. Bless us as we this day believe together for victory yet for Thy church around the earth. We give Thee praise through Christ Jesus our Lord.

Amen.

Love Without Control

Now Father, wilt Thou bless these words? We want to love Thee. We want to love Thy Son. We want to love the Holy Ghost. We want to love the Trinity until it becomes a delight. Until our Christianity ceases to be an escape, and becomes a mighty poured-out passion of enjoyable love.

Save us, we pray Thee our God. Save us from loving Thee for what we can get out of Thee. Help us to love Thee rather for what Thou art. O Jesus, Jesus, dearest Lord, we can't say, forgive me, if I say it for very love of Thy precious name, because that indicates that we're saying we love Thee so much we can control it. Lord, we control it pretty well. Forgive us Lord, because we can control it.

Forgive us, we pray, because we don't dance with joy. Forgive us because we're not like little children on Christmas morning. Forgive us that we're so cold-faced and staid and so poised and in control of ourselves. Help us to let go, and let go, until our love for Thee becomes a torrent, flowing like a torrent, rising like a fiery fountain. And Thou wilt love us in a measure that Thou canst now not do. Thou wilt manifest Thyself to us. And we walk all day and all night, and be all night with Thy love burning in our hearts. We'll be the tabernacle of the Most High God, the Shekinah, where the Deity dwells. My God, no angel, no angel could rise to that. No seraphim could top it. No cherub before the throne could rise higher.

Help us now, down on this earth, clothed in this clay tabernacle, to have such a burning fire within our bosoms, that people will find it out and know we love God. We ask it in Christ's name.

Amen.

Christian Success

Heavenly Father, we pray that Thou wilt single us out as though there weren't any others, and in lonely singleness speak to us. Lord, it isn't Thy will that we should fail in our Christian progress. Lead us, Lord. Thou hast spoken this morning. Of that we're quite certain. Continue to speak.

Save us, we pray Thee, from the result of our own foolishness. Save us from the traits of our own nature. Save us, we pray Thee, from our own laziness. And make this afternoon, for some, a time of crossing over. And now, may grace and mercy and peace in the Triune God, the Father, Son and Holy Ghost, be with us forever.

Amen.

A Clean Start

O Lord, our Lord, Thou knowest we are Thy sheep in the mountain. We are Thy little band of soldiers, surrounded by the enemy. And we don't want to waste our lives. We don't want to waste our money. We don't want to waste our time. We don't want to waste our gifts. Oh, we don't want to be as Peter and Didymus and the rest of them where they're sympathetic, friendly, believing in Thee, believing that Thou art risen, but not knowing what to do, because the Holy Ghost had not yet come. We don't want to simply follow some tall fellow who doesn't know what to do either, but because he's got a strong personality and good leadership, he says, "let's go do this." We don't want to waste our time and money and give up our precious, precious days following a man who's doing something he hasn't been sent to do. Lord, we'd rather join some little band of unheard-of, strange people somewhere, and live right and follow Thee, and be filled, and be right, than riding on the crest of popular religion.

Bless these friends, Lord, who listen tonight. They're here. They must want something or they wouldn't have come. God bless them. Jesus, take each one by the hand and lead us knee deep, knee deep in the succulent juicy pastures. Lead us, we pray Thee, to the still waters. Lead us, we pray Thee, on to the fulfillment of Thy promise, the promise of the Father.

Now, Lord, search us, search us—what we were, what we were yesterday or last year. That isn't anything, Lord. We'll start now. We'll start clean—now. We'll confess to Thee now. We'll ask Thee to pardon us now. Lord, Thou hast heard today, criticism. Thou hast heard today, whispered things. Thou hast seen today, tight mouths and set jaws as people passed each other. Thou hast heard today and seen and beheld the pride and the carnality.

O Lord Jesus, we don't hide anything and we don't deny anything. We confess it. As a people, as a church, we would confess. We would ask Thee to forgive. We would ask you to wash us whiter than the snow. And oh, that cleansing stream our sister sang about. That cleansing, that fountain, that overwhelming flood of cleansing power. Let it come to one after another of us. Save us, we pray, from the suave, smooth, get-along-with-everybody spirit. And help us to stand, we pray, with shining eyes and with full understanding of what it means to be a follower of Jesus.

Bless Thy people, Lord, in this great city. Bless every good man of God who stands to the care of the Truth. Bless him up to the light he has. Bless all the churches up to the light they have, and for everyone, we thank Thee. And for every poor sheep, we thank Thee. For every struggling, lean little lamb, we thank Thee. For everybody, Lord, that has looked longingly in Thy direction, we thank Thee, O Lord Jesus.

O Christ, Thou knowest the endless rat race, the constant wheel in the middle of a wheel, the buzzing, everlasting squirrel cage of empty activity. Come, Holy Spirit, heavenly dove. Come with all Thy quickening power. Come, shed abroad our Savior's love that it may quicken ours. If we're not lovable, forgive us. Help us to become lovable. Help us to become so people can love us without straining. Help us, Lord, so they won't have to be hypocrites to say they love us.

Bring us into a place where meekness and humility and tenderness and kindness and long-suffering shall prevail. Bring us into the thirteenth chapter of 1 Corinthians, Lord. It may cost us a lot. It's hard on the flesh. It's humbling, but there we know the mighty Holy Ghost will come. There, we know, He'll fall and keep falling and keep flowing down and in and out.

Gracious Lord, send us out of here tonight. Don't let anybody crack a joke at the door. Don't let anybody be so full of levity that they'll forget anything that's been said. Send us out, we pray Thee, to wonder about our responsibility to this very critical week that lies ahead of us. Mighty Lord, mighty Lord, the end of the ages is upon us. The world has grown old and the Judgment draws near, and kingdoms rising against kingdom, nation against nation. Evil men and seducers wax worse and worse and the love of many waxes cold. Thousands say, "Lord, Lord," but do not the things that Thou sayest.

Save this people, we pray Thee, from that quagmire. Save us, we pray Thee, from that hole in the swamp. And float us above it, like Noah in the Ark, riding above the storm. We ask this in Jesus' name.

Amen.

Walk Worthy

Now our Heavenly Father, our Father, who art in heaven. Thou knowest we're in a world of flesh, a world that, in the quaint language of old, is filled with janglers and pinchers and open praisers and blamers and triflers and curious persons—and the church has these in great abundance. Triflers and curious persons and tasters and experimenters and half in and half out, walking along, as Elijah said, on two unequal legs. Up today, down tomorrow, serving Baal with great fervency and then repenting and serving Jehovah the next week. Lord, the world is full of them and the churches are full of them!

O God, for Jesus' sake, wilt Thou not grant that we may move on into deeper spiritual things? That if we can't be a big and vast church, we can see born here some flaming evangels who will carry this message of discontent and spiritual longing with them wherever they go? And whose very testimony will put salt in the water of every saint and will put itch in their feet, and start them up on the high mountain pass toward the rarefied air, where the saints immortal dwell? Great God, wilt Thou help us now?

O Lord, this is our hope. Thy blood makes us worthy. This is my hope. If it were not so, Lord, if I did not know that Thy blood makes me worthy, I'd crawl off in a closet and let some more-worthy man try to present this Truth, that Thy blood makes us worthy. So in the worthiness of that blood we go forward, fearing no devil, no devil at all. No big devil, no little ones. No demons, nobody, nothing, fearing nothing. For Thy blood makes us worthy. And we thank Thee.

Now, thank Thee for this night's attendance here on this bitter night. And we pray Thee, Lord, if it please Thee, that over the next weeks we may speak to strategic persons. Send us the thirsty and the hungry. Keep, we pray Thee, the triflers and the curious away. And send the thirsting, and the hungry, and the longing, and the serious minded, and the eager, and those ready to confess their faults, and acknowledge their character blemishes, dispositional flaws—who won't defend themselves, but who will press on until they know Him and the power of His resurrection and of His cross. Until they shall go on toward the mark of the prize of the high calling of God in Christ Jesus.

We pray that out of this church there might come or might be born something that pleases Thee. There might be born something that was born in groups in olden times, when The Friends of God and the Brethren of the Common Life and Brethren of the Burning Hearts made the soil soft and ready for the coming of the great Reformers.

Graciously bless us. Send us out, we pray Thee, serious but happy—serious but not despondent. Knowing no matter how bad we are, there's hope in Jesus Christ: infinite, wonderful, infinite, glorious hope, in the blood of the Lamb. This we ask in Jesus' name.

Amen.

Crossing Over

O God, our Father, we pray tonight. We pray tonight that as we look over and see from this side of the river the wonderful hills of Canaan. We've been so long in the sand. Our feet, our shoes are full of sand, and we're dry and dusty and our eyes burn with the sand of evangelicalism. Over there, we see pomegranates on the tree. We see grapes, big grapes, on the vine. We see fat cattle. And we see trees and rocks, where bees are. And we see the green fertile fields. O Lord, we remember at Kadesh Barnea they turned back because they were afraid to go in.

Now, some of us have come up to Kadesh Barnea. And for some, there'll be the long, winding, interlacing journey, round and round and round in the sand. But we pray Thee that for others and for many, many others, there might be the willingness to cross over, to pass in, to open the Book, to kneel down, to search it, to follow it, to believe it, to obey, and to do what Thou sayest in that Word that we're to do.

Now, help us, Lord, this week to look on Thee steadily and at Thee alone. Not interfere with Thy workings. Not try to tell Thee how to run our lives, but look on Thee and at Thee alone. And this week, Lord, we want to be engaged, not with what we have, but with what we haven't yet. What we have, we leave with Thee. But what we haven't yet, we want to press forward toward it, gazing always at Thee. Let the gaze of the soul be ours this week.

Bless these people. For some it means a long trip in very ugly weather. Bless them this week. Bring them back. Give us, we beseech Thee, another wonderful time and very much further in than anything that we've had yet. We ask it in Christ's name. Amen.

Illuminate and Enlighten

O, blessed Lord Jesus, blessed Lord Jesus, we bless Thee tonight. We bless Thee tonight that Thou art our Lamb who died for our sins, our Priest and Advocate above. Thou art our head, and we the members of Thy body. Thou art the Lord of the church. Thou art the coming King of Israel. Thou art the coming King of the world. Ten thousand, thousand bright offices Thou dost have, and ten thousand virtues shine around Thy head.

O Lord, we remember that Thou wast in Eden, the garden of God. And that Thou wast in the garden and Adam heard the voice, the Word in the cool of the day. And we heard the Word thousands of years later, after that Word had been made flesh to dwell among us. But it's the same Word. We heard the Word.

We bless Thee tonight. We bless Thee in humility. In humility we come before Thee. We're ashamed of our sins. We're ashamed of every arrogant, proud, fleshly thing that shuts out the Light. Oh, illuminate our spirits. Raise what is low and illuminate what is dark, and enlighten, we beseech Thee, all that is obscure. And send us out, we beseech Thee, to be worshipers of the Most High God, maker of heaven and earth and Jesus Christ, His only Son, our Lord, and of the Holy Ghost the Comforter, who with the Father and Son together is worshiped and glorified. Make us that kind of Christian, Lord. The church, the modern Christianity has lots of the other kinds. Make us that kind of Christian, we pray. Oh, give us the culture of the Holy Ghost. Give us, we pray Thee, the deep spiritual learning of the Spirit.

And oh, we pray for Thy church, Lord, Thy evangelical church. We pray for Thy church all around, all over. The church, Lord God, that is caught in the world and that has been carried to Babylon and is in captivity, Lord, she has her Bible under her arm but she's still in captivity. She's hung her harp on the willows, because how can we sing the Lord's Psalms in Babylon. Great God, we pray Thou wilt revive Thy church again and reform us where we need reformation.

Send us a Luther, we pray Thee, and a Melanchthon, and Zwingli, and a Wesley and Finney. Send us, we pray Thee, men that will reform us, that will purify the church, that will give back to the church her ancient glory. Put the crown, which her Bridegroom gave her, upon her court again, that she may sit indeed as the bride of Christ. And instead of being like the world, she may be so beautifully unlike the world that the world will say, "Tell me, oh thou fairest among women. What is thy beloved more than another beloved, that we might find Him too? Show us where He is. Describe Him for us, because we're sick of love, we're sick seeing thy face, we've longed to have whatever made thy face shine."

Poor world. Lord God, we try to argue them in, and scare them into the kingdom, and scare them by Sputniks and bombs and all the rest. But oh, we pray Thee, may we be like the Bride of the Song of Solomon. That the daughters of Zion may come from everywhere and say, "Show us Thy Beloved, that we may follow Him too." Grant this, we pray, for Jesus' sake. We ask it in His Name.

Amen.

No Compromise

O Jesus, Jesus, Christ and Lord and King and Prince and Advocate and Priest and High Priest and Lamb that was slain. Someone pointed to Thee and said, "Behold the Lamb of God," and we followed Thee, and we thank Thee that Thou didst accept us and take away our sins. Then Thou didst say, "Now if you will follow me, take up your cross, deny yourself and follow me. And where I am, there my servant will be." Then began our compromising. Then we learned to make compromise, and we've learned it and become as skillful as a scholastic theologian. We've made ourselves comfortable and convenient.

O Lord Jesus, what shall we say to Thee? What shall we say to Thee? We send sixty-two percent of our income to the foreign field to make converts in Africa, Indonesia, South America, and the islands of the sea. Some of those same converts would be shocked if they came back and saw how cold we are. How full of jokes. How engrossed with the size of our automobiles and our rugs and our picture windows. My Lord Jesus, we are ashamed before Thee this day. We pray that Thou wilt help us to set our hearts like a flint, determinedly, and like Daniel, refuse to partake of the world's meats.

Help us, we pray, to hear Thy cheerful and encouraging voice, even after our disgraceful wanderings, say now, "Arise, rise, get up, move in. I'll be with you."

Gracious Lord, we pray Thee, touch every one of our hearts and tear away all of our little playhouses. Tear away, we pray Thee our God, all of the little idols that we've made unconsciously that we don't know we have, all the little comfortable pillows for our heads. Take them all away and bring us back down, as Jacob was to the rock.

Grant, we pray Thee, that there might be some serious heart searching during this week that lies ahead. Dear Savior, Thou knowest with rebellions and revolutions, and hydrogen bombs, and leagues of nations, Arab leagues, and the United Nations and the shaping up of things for the end times. And with man holding in his hand the weapon for suicide, Lord, we can't afford to play. Yet we're so well off, so monied, so comfortable, that we're learning to play. And we stretch ourselves on beds of ivory and invent instruments like David, and drink out of bowls and care not that the tread of the advancing enemy can be heard, though it shakes the earth, and the sound of the shout of the enemy is carried to us on every wind. And yet, we go our way.

My Father, help America. Help us of the fundamentalist churches. Help us of the gospel churches. Help us, we beseech Thee, help us. We have our Bibles and we claim to believe, but O Father, so did the Pharisees. We beseech Thee, help us to put our beliefs to practice. Let it cost us something, we beseech Thee.

Now, we're trusting, we pray, for our people that are out and gone and away, many of them, and they'll be back tomorrow. They'll be back in time to work, but they didn't get back in time for church today, but bless them anyway, Lord, and help them, and let them not leave their bones on the highways. Have mercy upon these poor people who are traveling in bumper-to-bumper, long lanes of traffic coming into the city tonight. Let there be fewer and no accidents and preserve lives. We don't deserve it, but have mercy on us for Jesus Christ's sake. Put into the hands of the right people the right literature. We beseech Thee that we may break out of this conventional shell of dead level of mediocrity and break through into courageous, daring, unusual, radical, if need be, kind of spiritual lives that our frightened friends call us fanatics.

But Thou wilt smile, as Thou dost see that we are pushing on into the land which Thou hast promised us in Christ Jesus, spiritual places, the heavenly places, with which we've been blessed, but about which we do so little. We ask all this in Christ's name.

Amen.

Spared to Serve

"The LORD reigneth, he is clothed with majesty; the LORD is clothed with strength, wherewith he hath girded himself: the world also is stablished, that it cannot be moved. Thy throne is established of old: thou art from everlasting. The floods have lifted up, O LORD, the floods have lifted up their voice; the floods lift up their waves. The LORD on high is mightier than the noise of many waters, yea, than the mighty waves of the sea. Thy testimonies are very sure: holiness becometh thine house, O Lord, forever" (Ps. 93).

Now we would this morning, Father, join the psalmist, and with ten thousand and thousands of thousands who worship Thee this morning and with the spirits of just men made perfect, and with the General Assembly and Church of the First Born whose names are in heaven, we would unite and add our tiny little sound to the sound that's like the sound of many waters, praising and worshiping Thee, the God and Father of our Lord Jesus Christ, who made us and who pitied us, and who sent Thy Son to redeem us, and who waits to receive us in the day when we shall have redemption completed in us. And Thy work of glorification shall make us worthy to gaze upon Thy face.

Now, our Father, we join to ask Thy mercy upon our world. We join to ask Thee, O God, to spare us, to spare the reckless, to spare the worldly and the careless. To spare those who today will not darken the door of any church, who have not thought one holy thought today and will not during the whole day, but who will indulge in everything the flesh can offer them and will have no thought of death or judgment or the world to come. We do not scold them, nor do we come before Thee and say we're not as other men. We are just as other men and we are all alike, O God. But Thou hast in great mercy found some of us and made us want to love Thee, and made us want to be right, and made us want to serve Thee in a world where the service costs us something.

Father, we pray that Thou wilt bless our country. Bless the land that Thou gavest to our fathers who came from bondage beyond the sea to establish a church here that would be free. Father, we thank Thee for our land. We thank Thee for our country. We pray that Thou wilt bless it and bless those who are in authority in it.

We pray for the health of the people, the leaders of the church. We pray God for Bible schools and for seminaries and Christian colleges and missions and church schools, and great churches and small churches, and celebrated pastors and evangelists and men who are obscure and little heard of but who love Thee as sincerely and as truly as those whose names are on everybody's lips. Bless Thou all over today, our Father.

Breathe Thy breath of life-giving power and animating grace upon the church that's fighting and struggling and having a hard time, but still is going on. Bless behind the Iron Curtain. Bless behind bamboo curtains and all curtains, for it's difficult to pray. God, bless Thou our Christian brethren who are caught in the terrible grind of communism. We pray, bless the church, Thy church, and hasten the hour when the Holy Son shall return to glorify the living and raise the dead and make us like unto Himself. This we ask through Jesus Christ our Lord.

Amen.

Strength in Weakness

Father, we pray that Thou wilt bless us through the Word. We thank Thee for this picture gallery which stood in front of this great big man, Samson. We love him and we pity him. What he might have been and what he was are such sharp contradictions, and the warning to the centuries. O Lord, if we could never be as strong as he was, let us not be as weak as he was. If we never could be great, we pray Thee, help us that we might reverently cultivate the little plant that we do have. We ask it, in Christ's name.

Amen.

PENITENTIAL

IN HIS IMMANENCE, GOD HAS boundless enthusiasm. He's enthusiastic for Himself in the persons of the Godhead. The persons of the Godhead are infinitely delighted with each other. The Father is infinitely delighted with the Son, and the Son is infinitely delighted with the other two persons of the Godhead. He is delighted with His whole creation, and especially for men made in His image. Unfortunately, for us as sinful people unbelief comes in and throws a cloud over us and shuts out the light of God. We don't believe what's actually here, that God is delighted, infinitely delighted with us. Understanding this, we can come boldly and confidently to Him in prayer.

Here's a little prayer that was once made. O God, of Thy goodness, give me Thyself, for Thou art enough to me and I may ask nothing that is less. God, give me Thyself.

When we pray for revival, real revival, it must begin by saying, O God, give me Thyself, for nothing less than Thee will do, or anything less than God. Anything less than God, Julian of Norwich says, ever me wanteth. I like that little expression. Everything from the proton to the farthest, remotest heavenly body, up and down the scale, all the beautiful things of earth and sky and sea and all the diamonds of the mines and all timber of the forest and all the charm of the landscape and all the riches of the cities. If I have it all and have not Thee, ever me wanteth. Translated into modern English, it means, O God, it won't be enough. It won't be enough.

Do you know, deep down, what's the matter with everybody? Nobody will say it, and the average person wouldn't believe it, but there's a little shrine inside of you. There's a shrine so far in that nobody can know that shrine but you. There is a penetralium, a deep, deep shrine, far eastward in Eden. And it lies in that great soul of yours. And there's a shrine there and a garden and a throne. No matter what you get, there'll be a cry from that shrine, ever me wanted, O God, I'm still hungry. God, I'm still hungry. Give men everything. As the song said it, take the world but give me Jesus. We can have all the world and have not Jesus. And still, there's a cry from deep within, ever me wanteth.

I think the greatest calamity for a human soul is to be made in the image of God, and to be made with a spirit so big that it can contain the universe and cry for more. That it's bigger than the heavens and the heaven of heavens, and be empty of God and yet go through the eternity to come crying, ever me wanteth, O God, forever and forever.

Useful and Holy

Dear Lord Jesus, there are about twenty people who desire us to pray for them. We would unite our hearts and come as one, so we were all one. And Thy servant who's praying out loud, dear Lord Jesus, will join myself to all these who stand.

We would pray together tonight, Lord, please do something in us and for us. Please Lord, the collective soul is cold and our hearts are so loveless. And the thought of sin is so common and our longing after Thee is so weak. We're ashamed all the way around. That we see, Lord, that if we're going to make any spiritual progress, were going to have to lay bare our chest and say, "Wound me, O Thou lover of my soul, faithful friend. Wound me unto death and raise me to newness of life."

We pray for these all. We beseech Thee, Lord, that Thou would take these friends on with Thee step by step into the deep things of the Bible. Make these friends, we pray Thee, a core—a hard, central core and nucleus on which can be built a larger group that can catch from them the fever of longing after God, that can catch from them the compassion, that can catch from them the right attitude towards sin and their own past.

O Lord, we thank Thee for forgiven sin. We'll never have to face it again. But we don't want carelessly to forget, Father, we've been sinners, so wound us. We beseech Thee, give us compassion that if it takes away our happiness, all right, Lord. We don't care about being happy. We want to be useful and holy.

And then, Lord, our love, longing after Thee, that's jubilant pining and longing for Thee. Fill our hearts with it, O Lord, until all hours, whatever we're doing and may be in our hearts always the up-springing of loving desire.

Grant Thee, we beseech, that these persons who requested prayer may have this in such measure as will astound them and will make great, useful, powerful Christians out of them. Grant this for Jesus' sake.

Repent and Believe

Our Father, we pray, we would repent before Thee this morning. Lord, rather than just pray, we would repent before Thee, O Lord, for our materialistic mindset, thinking in terms of this world—judging, weighing, measuring, valuing as men do. Father, this is wrong. Forgive us.

And Father, our preoccupation with earthly things also, we would repent this morning. As a people we would repent, for our absorption in the things that pass away. O Lord, forgive us, cleanse us, wash us, so that as we quiet our hearts, and in silence hear a voice, we may not have on us the ragged lint and dust of unconfessed sin, that our garments may be white this morning—pure and shining, that we may receive. Unworthy, but believing people.

Break the bread of life this morning, O Thou Bread of Life. Break it, wine of the soul, spill it. Feed us until we want no more. In Jesus' holy name.

Amen.

In Wrath, Remember Mercy

O Christ, here we are. After nineteen-hundred and fifty years. Here we are. We claim to be Thy followers. O Christ, there's so much of us and so little of Thee. So much of earth and so little of heaven. So much that can be explained and so little that can't be. Oh, so much of the human mind and so little of the Holy Ghost.

We apologize before Thy Majesty. We repent before the throne of Thy glory. We cry tonight, O God, forgive us our sins, and pardon our guilt, and cleanse our pollution, and deliver us from ourselves, and excuse and forgive, we pray Thee, the human, nearly human element that we have thought was divine, the sweat that we thought was spirit. The buoyancy that we thought was the Holy Ghost. O God, what this has done to our country. What it's done to religion. What it's done, Lord, we apologize for Thee and for the Holy Spirit. We've tried to please everybody and fit into society, and the result is we are being pushed back and a "virgin" is now walking the streets and being in big glass cases and carried around and exhibited.

They're trying to put her on our stamps, boldly pushing in.

Lord, in another generation we'll be on our knees to idols in America. And it's our fault. We've promoted human imitations instead of the divine reality. We have not had Thee in our minds and Thou art taking revenge against us. We would not have Mary's Son, so you're allowing them to give us Mary. We wouldn't have the Holy Ghost, so they're giving us holy water. And we're being pushed back, shut up, and intimidated. And the newspapers are being chained and speakers and radio commentators are all afraid to talk. Everybody's afraid to dare to rise against this great and unfaithful Babylon.

My Lord God, it's a judgment on us, a judgment! For we've been converted without repentance, born again without faith, accepted Thee—it is so called—without revolution. O Lord, we've done it. We've sinned—the churches, ourselves, we preachers. My God, this night, wilt Thou not help us? Wilt Thou not revive us again in the midst of the years and in wrath? Remember mercy, O Lord. And we pray, give wisdom and insight to the leadership in America once more, we pray.

O God, we pray, give us prophets again in leadership—prophets in our pulpits—fearless, terrible men. Multiply the Ravenhills and the Reidheads and the Wellses. Multiply these men, O God, who don't care for anything, and who wouldn't run from ten devils if they met them in an alley. Raise up such terrible men in this frightful hour, we pray Thee, O God.

My God, we see timid pastors, cowardly, feminine. Forgive us, Lord, O God, and put the oil of the prophet on our heads and on the heads of young men coming up. As we are coming out of council next Wednesday, Lord, and with a week from tomorrow there will be elections and board members chosen, and a president chosen, O God, please Lord, don't take revenge on us as a society and give us a tabby cat as a president. Give us a prophet, God. O God, these clawless, toothless, soft, silky tabbies that have learned the soft religious phrases of so sweet and loving in the wind and love them and they're so nice. But my God, what traitors to the kingdom they are! Save us, we pray, from the traitors, and give us men of courage, Elijahs and bold Zedekiahs, and strong men, Zachariahs and Isaiahs and Moses and such men as that. We pray Thee, give us sons of thunder as John Knox and Finney and Sam Jones and Luther. O Lord, we beseech Thee.

Redeemed from Shame

O God our Father, we thank Thee. We thank Thee. We thank Thee for Jesus Christ Thy Son. We haven't done anything that we can think of but what we're ashamed of. We haven't got anything but what we ought to be ashamed of. We haven't got anything—our brains, our minds, our bodies, our souls, our spirits. We haven't done anything ourselves except what Thou hast given us. What Thou hast given us, we're not ashamed of and we're glad for, and we're deeply grateful for.

And we will go and appear and be there, dressed in Thy righteousness alone, faultless to stand before the throne. Thou wilt know us and claim us and not be ashamed of us because we were redeemed in Thy mercy—poor, scarred, bruised, pathetic, pale-faced, dying. Thou didst find us and save us and lift us and renew us and give us life, and we're Thine.

Would Thou bless this congregation? And we pray for any who may not be saved, that they may see what they're missing and turn quick to Jesus Christ, and say, "Lord, I am sorry for my past. From here on I'm Thine." Gracious Lord, bless us as we sing now at the close of the service. In Christ's name.

Amen.

Follow the Lamb

Now, Father, we pray for these men who've requested us to pray. Oh, Thou knowest the flesh. Thou knowest the temptation of the Adamic lion to rise and try to have its way by force. And we know how utterly necessary it is that we should learn the way of the Lamb that won by dying. It lives because He died and lives forevermore. Oh, Thou hast called us to follow the Lamb, not the lion. Thou didst never say follow the man but Thou hast said, these followed the Lamb, followed the Lamb. So we would follow the Lamb.

Help these who requested prayer this night. Teach them not only the doctrine of this, but teach them deeply and inwardly, far in, deep in, how to live as the saints of old lived, in humility. As Paul lived, who, when he inadvertently spoke against the High Priest, he immediately apologized and said, "I'm sorry, I didn't know he was the High Priest." O God, we pray Thee, teach us the beauty of apology and confession. Teach us, we pray Thee, the power of meekness and teach us the strength of weakness. Graciously bless us as we wait upon Thee in Christ's name.

Amen.

Standing in Need

O God, God our Father, Thou knowest we're followers of Thy Son. We know we are and we're not backing out, and we're not allowing the devil to tell us we aren't. We know we are. We're known of Him because we know Him. And we bless Thee.

But oh, Thou knowest, Father, the chronic non-expectation. Dear Lord, we are as Israel was in some measure anyhow. We don't expect anything from Thee. We pray and pray and pray and pray the same words, Wednesday after Wednesday and expect nothing. Forgive us, Lord, forgive us. For all these who now stand saying, pray for me, I do lift up my heart to Thee and pray for myself too, O God.

Oh, Thou knowest, Father, how easy it is to get into a mental rut. So easy to let yesterday dictate tomorrow and let things that were decide things that will be. Thou hast said Thou art a God who maketh all things new. We pray that Thou wilt touch the hearts of all these friends and give them a faith that will rise and dare to believe Thee to do the unexpected, and even the impossible. For Thou art the God of the impossible. O God, break out, even over the next days upon us here, in such measure and such fullness that Satan will begin to feel ajar. That he'll know, that he'll know that he's not running things. He'll know that Thou hast risen! Bare Thy mighty arm, O God, and give us faith to trust Thee that we may not grieve Thee by our chronic unbelief.

Now Father, we ask that Thou wilt bring us to the house of God tonight after an afternoon of penitence and waiting on Thee. Bring us to the house of God tonight. Bring in others and give us a wonderful, refreshing, glorious time together. And now, may grace and mercy and peace from the Triune God, the Father, Son and Holy Ghost be with us forever.

Amen.

Ready and Waiting

O God, Thou knowest how the world has sinned. How Thy people have sinned. How we've forgotten that we're made for another world. We put our trust in civilization. We put our trust in the principles of Abraham Lincoln and Gladstone and Bismarck and the rest of them. And we've forgotten that only Thy holy Son can bring peace to the world.

Help us, we pray, to live in a world that's on the brink, always on the brink, and to live separated and clean and pure and expectant. And help us to keep, so that if Thou dost come for Thy people before the heel of Antichrist tramples on the nations of men, we'll be ready. We'll be ready, Lord, not surfeiting and not drunk, not all bogged down in things, that we'll be as Israel was in Egypt, with our loins girded about and our staff in our hand and our light burning, ready to go.

Bless this company, we pray Thee. Keep Thy hand upon us. Give us a good week. Give a safe journey to our homes and let Thy blessing rest upon us through Jesus Christ our Lord.

Amen.

Pressing On

We are assembled here tonight, Lord Jesus. It's Thy disciples. Thy servant has tried, from the New Testament and from the Old, to explain the way of power and life. Now, Lord, Thou knowest how much easier it is to stand up here and explain it than it is to go out tomorrow and live it. And yet, it's possible to live it, otherwise Thy Word would be confusion, more confounded.

We pray, O Christ, while the church goes on, without power, without holiness, without radiance, plugging along. We thank Thee, Father, for every one that's plugging along. Thank Thee, Father, for everyone that says any good thing about Thy Son. We thank Thee for everyone whose testimony, whether hollow, still may be on Thy side. We remember Thy servant who said, "I thank God that Christ is preached, regardless of how He is preached." So we're glad for everybody, but O Lord, we mourn the weakness, the carnality, the selfishness that's in Thy church, among Thy people. We mourn that we don't grow up, that we don't advance. We stay little when we could be great Christians. O Lord, help us now.

Father, we pray for those who have requested it. Thou hast said "pray one for another" and there's a reason for Thy saying that. So we pray Thee for these who have said "pray for me," men and women. We pray for them. We pray that they may tear themselves loose. If they have to do it, do it by violence, from the green briars and the barbed wire, and get themselves out of all that, and escape the snares and traps of the flesh and follow Christ. And by faith, put themselves with Him on a cross and see themselves rise with Him into glorious light and freedom. Grant this, we pray.

Lead these dear friends on. Put the right books in their hands. Lead them to the right scripture. Help them to find time during the day or night that they ordinarily don't have to settle some of these things privately. Grant it, we pray. And let this, we pray Thee, spread not only here to these who raised their hands, but all among Thy children.

Begin, we pray Thee, O God, soon to draw a line between the swaggering, smiling, self-assured, self-confident, bold Christians, and the lowly and the meek and the humble and the merciful who deny self and follow Thee. Let the Holy Ghost come upon some people, the humble, the lowly, the crucified, that they may rise to newness of life to shine and be an example to the ones that aren't. Let it be so we pray in the name of Jesus Christ our Lord.

Amen.

8

THANKFULNESS

GOD IS THE PERFECT CREATOR and He runs everything by being present in His works. That's all throughout the Old Testament in the prophets and the Psalms and the book of Job. When we hit the age of science, we forgot that and we have laws now. The Bible knew nothing about the laws of nature, but only that God was there. If it rained, it was God watering His mountains from His upper chambers. If there was lightning, it was God, and if it thundered, it was the voice of the Almighty. God was always there. They were acutely God-conscious. And so, they were never lonely, because God was there. "God was in this place and I knew it not," said the man Jacob.

This idea that God is an absentee engineer, running His universe by remote control, is all wrong. He is present in perpetual and continuous eagerness with all the fervor of rapturous love pressing His holy design. Now you say, but I haven't felt that way about it. Well, it's unbelief that makes you feel otherwise. It's preoccupation with this world. If you would believe God, you would know this to be true. I would like to point out that God can't feel indifferent about anything. People are indifferent, but God isn't indifferent. God either loves with a boundless unremitting energy, or He hates with consuming fire. The goodness of God is the reason for existence, the reason and the explanation for things, the reason underlying all things. The goodness of God is the only reason for it.

Why does God answer prayer? Let's not imagine that it's because somebody was good enough. We Protestants think we don't believe in saints. Oh, we believe in saints all right. We don't canonize them twenty-five years after they're dead, but we put an "St." behind them. We don't do that, but we do canonize them. And we have St. George Mueller, and St. Spurgeon and St. Moody and St. Simpson, all Protestant saints. We get the idea that God answered prayer for them because they were real good. They would deny that fervently if they were here. Every one of them would deny it.

And yet, no one has ever received a thing from God on the grounds that he deserved it. How therefore could a human race that hadn't existed deserve something? How could a man who wasn't yet created earn anything or pile up any merit? He deserves only punishment and death.

So, if God answers prayer, it's because God is good. The answer is, God, of His goodness thought of it. God, of His goodness, out of His lovingkindness, His good-natured benevolence, God answers prayer. So remember, God is the source of everything. It was the goodness of God, the loving kindness of God. Because God, out of His goodness, acts according to that goodness and does what His loving heart dictates that He do.

Protected by Providence

Lord Jesus, we thank Thee this evening that we ever were created at all. We might lie tonight in the empty, forgotten void with an unremembered past. But Thou didst speak to nature and say, "Bring forth," and we are here. Lord, we think of these youngsters who escaped death, though narrowly, on the road. And then we remember that probably each one here—each of us—would have to say, if he knew all the facts, "I escaped death by a hair breadth a thousand times."

O Lord, we thank Thee that after we were born and Thou didst say "Bring forth," nature brought us forth, and Thy providence protected us all these years. We're scarred a little and we show a few bumps here and there like an old car—a ding here and a rusty spot there—but we're still holding together. Grace has preserved us. What grace did in our birth, grace has done in our providential protection.

And we thank Thee, O God, that Thou didst think of a way to redeem us when we would sin. To save us when we were lost. To find us when we're perishing. By grace we're Thine, those of us that are Thine; by infinite grace, unqualified grace, we are Thine.

Oh, we pray tonight, our Father, for our families. It's Christmas season when we're getting cards and presents and sending them. Telephone calls and telegrams and families that are broken, they're being united for a brief, happy hour. We remember the loved ones. To think of them now, boys brought up in this church, some of them girls. The church was too little for them and too narrow and the world was too big and the practicing is gone. O God, hear us while we pray for our lost relatives. Remember this season and keep Thine eye upon them. Do anything you have to do to get them saved.

Greatest Discovery

Lord, we thank Thee. We thank Thee for the faith once delivered. We thank Thee for all the music and poetry and artistry, all the high flights of the religious spirit, all the dreams of holy men and the visions of sage and seer. We thank Thee for the places that are marked to remind us of men who once walked on earth, good men and true, faithful men and true.

Then, we thank Thee that all their activities in faith and belief and discipline and prayer and warfare all led us to Him, who is His fulfillment. Now, we found Him. We have found Him, this man who told us everything we ever did. This wondrous Man, who never sinned, who would sit and talk to us, who never did anything else but sin. How we thank Thee for this miracle. This wonderful shining miracle of the Man who came from men. Blessed Jesus, receive our thanks. We thank Thee, Lord, we thank Thee.

We pray that Thou wilt help everybody here tonight to open

his heart, her heart, wide to the Savior. And to believe that He will come in instantly and at once. And plant a well there, and spring up, and spring up, and spring up, on and on while the ages go by, up unto eternal life. Lord, help us. Help any who may be on the borderline tonight. Help any who may be partly backslidden. Help any who may be wandering. Help any who may be doubting.

May we beseech Thee this night. May there be a quick turning of the spirit to the God of spirits who seeketh such to worship Him, these who worship in spirit and in truth. We ask it in Jesus' holy name.

Amen.

Grateful and Satisfied

O God our Father, it's with a good deal of joy and pleasure that we own ourselves members of the human race. Thou didst make man in Thine image. In sin accepted, Thou art not ashamed of what Thou hast made. We're not ashamed of ourselves, only of our sin.

O God, we're glad we're humans. We're glad that we stand up on the earth and don't walk and bark. We don't fly around, make nests or swim in the sea. We're glad we're humans. Glad we're created in Thine image to stand upright, to think and remember, to sing, make music and art. But our imaginations roam and create things. We're glad we're human, Father. Thank Thee, Heavenly Father, we were ever born of woman. Then, Father, in deep reverence, there are those that can say in utter humility, we thank Thee also that we were born again.

Out of the Fall of Adam's race, out of the lost and the wretched, distressful condition, Thou didst bring us by redemption. And now, we're born another time. Now, this time, into Thine image again, to be like Thee, not externally, but internally. By continual process of perfection until when we shall see Thee, we shall be like Thee, and Thy name shall be on our forehead.

Oh, we thank Thee we that are Christian. Thank Thee. Father, we want Thee to know that we're not satisfied. We're not as good of Christians that we want to be. And there are flaws in us that even our unsaved friends notice. And they look across and sneer and say, "Who are you to say you're in an upper kingdom when you live in a way that I know it's got a fault in it?" And we don't deny it, Lord. We admit it. We Christians, tonight, here in this church now, this audience, we admit it, Father, that there are yet imperfections and flaws in Adam's old flesh. But, O Lord Jesus, we're looking to Thy blood and we're looking to Thy Spirit and we're looking to the fire of the Holy Ghost to purge and to perfect and change and sanctify and purify until, little by little, it'll come until men will not have any fault to find with us. But they'll say, surely God is among them as a truth.

But oh, we thank Thee for this new kingdom, a kingdom of the Spirit. We thank Thee for all those saints from whom all their labor rest. Thank you for all the saints we know and all that we don't know, scattered everywhere that had been born of the Spirit and washed in the blood, who call Christ Savior and God Father, and who are aligned tonight.

Now we pray Thee for those who by every test and all classifications, by every distinguishing mark, know that they are only Adam's seed. They don't belong to Thee. Thou art not their Father. Christ is not their Savior. Heaven is not their home. Eternal life is not their destiny and they know it. God, we pray for them. We pray that they may come and believe in Jesus Christ, and accept the witness of the Lord and Savior. Believe what He tells them, identify themselves with Him morally, cast in their lot with Him, and follow the Lamb. Oh, grant it, Father, for Jesus' sake. Grant it, Father, in Jesus' Name.

Amen.

Mission Possible

O blessed Lord Jesus, blessed Lord Jesus, Thou didst come on a mission. Our trembling hearts tell us Thou shouldst have come with blazing eyes to be our Judge. Thou shouldst have come as our executioner to put to death such moral vermin that's crawled over the face of the earth, polluting each other and ourselves. But Thou didst not come to condemn the world. Thou didst come that the world, through Thee, might be saved. What can we say, Lord, but thank Thee, O Gentle Savior. How can we borrow language to thank Thee for this, Thy dying sorrow and pity without end.

We thank Thee, Lord Jesus. Lord Jesus, we won't fight about Thee and we won't argue about hypotheses. We will only kneel and say, "My Lord and my God." We have found Him of whom Moses and the Prophets did write. Jesus, the son of Mary, the Son of God. We have found Him. Hallelujah! We have found Him. We thank Thee.

We pray for the friends present tonight. We thank Thee for those who responded last week. Lord, we praise Thee tonight, Thou wilt grant that there may be those who will go out of this place now with a solemn, lasting conviction that this means the personal individual person, the one, knowing, knowing, knowing, that was for them, He came this way. Blessed Jesus, help us as we wait upon Thee just a little longer tonight. In the name of Christ.

Amen.

Bonded in Fellowship

Bless the Lord, oh my soul. We worship Thee, crowned with life. We worship Thee, who makest the wind Thy chariot and who stretches forth the curtains of the heavens as a tent to dwell in. We would unite in worshiping Thee. Lord of all being, whose glory flames from sun and star. We bless Thee this day.

We thank Thee for every good grace which has come to us. We thank Thee for obstacles and hindrances, disciplines, and hard places as well. We thank Thee, Lord, for every twinge of pain we've suffered. We thank Thee for every thrill of delight we've known. We thank Thee and worship Thee, the Father Almighty, Father of an infinite Majesty, Thine adorable and only Son Jesus Christ our Lord. We worship also the Holy Ghost who, with the Father and the Son, is worshiped and glorified.

We pray Thy blessing upon us, this company of friends. The personnel of the company change from year to year. Its duties and necessities call us to separate and scatter to all parts of the United States and the world. Now we pray for our friends as they leave us today, going to establish residence in a new part of our country. We thank Thee that there will be no breaking the circle of fellowship, but the family remains intact—the family called after Thee, the Father of Lights and the Heavenly Father of all the families of earth, the circles of redeemed families who trust in Thy Son. Wilt Thou bless them?

Please bless this brother in his preaching ministry and this sister as the wife of an important missionary man. Bless them all. We trust Thee, our Father, that the grace that has kept them up to now will continue to keep them. Bless all the people who need

Thy help, friends and relatives and kin, these who worship here.

O God, graciously bless us. Give us a sense of worship that will be finer and grander than any earthly thing. Help in the preaching of the Word. Help, we pray Thee, as we sing these great songs together. Bless our country, our president, the people of the earth, the poor, staggering United Nations, and those, O Lord, upon whose shoulders rests the weight of government. Help Lord, but we need Thee so desperately in these critical hours of the world's history. We commit ourselves to Thee through Jesus Christ our Lord.

Amen.

Delightful Discovery

God, God our Father, we bless Thee. It would take us all to-night to tell Thee how wondrous Thou art. And the books haven't been written. Not enough hymns or anthems have been composed to tell what our hearts owe Thee. We've searched and reached out and struggled for that which was, for the unseen, the substance, the essence, the being, and lo, to our delight, we have found that He is our Father.

"When you pray say, our Father, which art in heaven, hallowed be Thy name." We thank Thee that our hearts have found you, the Lord of all being. Before Thy ever-blazing throne, we ask no luster of our own. Send these Christians out to be evangelists and soul winners in their own right. Send them out, we pray Thee, ablaze with this, to tell their sinner relatives and friends and neighbors what Jesus Christ can do for the returning soul. We ask it in His holy name.

Amen.

A Mighty Purgation

God our Father, God our Father, Thou hast made us and we're glad. Glad we were ever born. Glad our tired mothers ever brought us into the world. Glad that we ever saw the sunrise. Glad that we learned to speak and see and hear. Glad, O God, we're glad we're alive. Glad we're human beings, not earthworms or bugs. Glad Thou didst make us in Thine image. Oh, we're glad tonight.

Father, we've sinned, we've suffered, we've disappointed Thee and disappointed our friends. We've disappointed ourselves, tumbled around, and we can look far down the mountain where we wandered many years—often troubled in our journey by the ghosts of doubt and fears. And it's all true of us. But we thank Thee for redemption in His blood. We thank Thee for the best and dearest Father who loved us and who loves, and who in pollution saved us from our pollution, saved and delivered us. We thank Thee, thank Thee, Lord, tonight for redemption. We thank Thee for redemption.

Now Father, for these eight persons who've asked us to pray. Father, wilt Thou search them as with a candle? Wilt Thou search them as with a candle? And grant, our Father, we pray Thee, that before they close their eyes and sleep tonight, that any doubt they have will be swept away as the billows of the sea sweep things from rocks, as the wind in its fury sweeps away the leaves, sweep away from their hearts. Cleanse, we pray Thee, by a mighty purgation, whatever hinders them. Take away, we pray Thee, those heavy weights that load them down, and put within them by the new birth, we pray Thee, the magnet that feels the tug of Jerusalem above.

Great God, we pray for all these friends. We pray that this week they won't let their work and eating and sleeping and drinking and bathing and talking and reading the newspaper— they will not let those things hinder them from seeking Thy face with an urgency and fervor they've never known before. But pray Thou wilt deliver from habits. That Thou wilt go through, O Lord, and purge and let the fiery purgation of the Holy Ghost cleanse their hearts. Let the blood roll over their souls and deliver them so that whatever comes, life or death, they'll know that they belong up there, and that there is a vacuum up there waiting for them into which they will rush, sweetly, beautifully when they die.

God, if there be those here tonight and any of those who raised a hand, might they know in their deep, honest hearts tonight that the magnetic pulls downward, we pray Thee, God, make a change this night. No later, Lord; we can't afford to wait. Now, we commit them to Thee.

And now Father, we join to pray for this boy who was ill who was brought here from Lombard. We pray for his physical deliverance. It is written that they shall lay hands on the sick and they shall recover. Lord, we've been afraid of that and we have shied away from it. But it's there and we're Thy believers and we're Christians. And we have a right to believe, Lord, that when Thou dost offer us something, that we're supposed to take it. Wilt Thou bless us? And as we later gather a little group to pray, oh, come on us with the gift of faith and of prayer that we might pray the prayer of faith.

Amen.

Heavenly Hearing

O God, we thank Thee for the singing in which we hear a sound that isn't earthly. It's neither the cheap song of the world, nor is it the fine classical song of the world, but there's another voice. We hear it, and it harmonizes with the beasts and elders and living creatures and ransomed who, with palms in their hands, stand at the sea and sing together of Him who loved them and washed them in His own blood.

We're glad to hear this, Lord, and know what it will be

like, a little bit of it at least. We thank Thee for an assembly of Christians. We thank you for this church. We thank Thee for this crowd here this steamy night. And Lord, it isn't the largest church on the continent, but to us, the dearest and the most important, and we pray that Thou wilt grant that tonight there may go forth truth that will be helpful to people. Some don't need it; some are on their way. Some have long past the necessity for any of my preaching. The younger ones are coming up, new ones are coming in. Many others, by the scores, are going to other parts of the country and other parts of the world and taking the instruction and the message with them there. New ones are hearing. God, grant, we pray tonight, that in utter humility and consciousness, that it is not "I" and not man and not the voice of man, but the voice of the Spirit. May we hear Thee.

Speak, O Lord Jesus. Grant mercy to be over us. Bless this hot, noisy, jumpy city with its cacophonous rackets and its fears and its lusts and its deceptions and its lies and its demon possession. O God, have mercy on this great concentration of evil we name Chicago. We thank Thee Thou hast in it a number who haven't bowed the knee to Baal or kissed his image and never will. Thank Thee for them, Father. We are thankful some of them are here tonight. Graciously help us, that it may be in power, and not in word only. In Christ's name.

Amen.

Grateful for Light

Father, we pray first, we want to thank Thee that we have light on this. We want to thank Thee that in Thy infinite mercy, Thou hast not let us go like cattle to the slaughter, not knowing where we're going, and because we're fat and sleek, imagining that we're all right, when actually we've been fattened for the slaughter. We thank Thee, Lord, that we've got a light on this. Now, help us to walk in. Bless us, every one. Take away all false hopes and all unscriptural expectations and pull us back to the Word of the Lord.

O Father, out as we go down the steps and onto the sidewalk tonight and mark the forehead of them that the sign cries. Great God, have mercy upon our America. Have mercy, we pray, upon our America with its dozens of gods, at least a dozen gods. Have mercy, Father, and help us to turn from idols to serve Thee and to wait for Thy Son from heaven. Dismiss us now. We ask in the name of Jesus Christ our Lord.

Amen.

Journey to Eternity

O Father, if anybody is saved here tonight, we want publicly to confess that it's because of Thy goodness and not because of our deserving it. Thou didst think of it first. We thought we thought of it first, but we didn't. Thou didst call us before we ever turned an ear. Oh, we thank Thee. What has anybody here that we didn't receive? We were paupers, beggars, tramps, until we heard the Voice. I heard the voice of Jesus say, come unto me and rest. Oh, we thank Thee, Lord. We heard it. We heard the voice of Jesus say, "I am this dark world's Light. Come unto me, Thy morn shall rise and all Thy day be bright." Blessed Jesus, we thank Thee we heard it. O God, a good, kind, friendly, gentlemen of a brother didn't hear it; he isn't hearing it yet.

My God, what have we, what have we? Oh, who is sufficient for these things? Thou in Thy goodness hast done these things for us. Lord, we pray Thee for those who have felt a tug of the Spirit this night. May they not allow their eyes to close in slumber until they have closed with the gospel message, until they have turned to Jesus Christ. And them that turn to Him will not be cast out, but be received. Oh, wilt Thou help us here now?

O God, we pray for these who've requested prayer this night, but we'd take them by the hand and then lead them in, but it's not a journey for the feet, so we can't lead them by the hand. It's a journey for the heart, and only the Holy Ghost can lead the heart. So lead these hearts. Lead them, Lord. These men and this woman. Lead their hearts, to the blood-stained cross, to the foot of Calvary. The place where all sinners have to begin. The place where eternal life is found, or at the open grave where Christ the Lord has risen, and gives eternal life to all that God has given Him.

Bless these friends, all of them. Now help us as we go to our homes. Lord, we'll have a long, tough week if we live, all of us. It will be cold. It will be bad underfoot. There'll be disturbing news of plane crashes. Lots of evil things as even we've heard today. There'll be threats out of Moscow. There will be evidences of iniquity among young people, wolf packs and crime waves. There will be trouble in the factories and shops and offices. Oh, we pray that Thou wilt help us to rise above it all on the wings of faith, and to live in Thy heart so far and deep that we'll scarcely know we're down here. We'll only know that we're Thine and Thou art ours. Definitely, we commit to Thee those who've requested prayer. We believe we're heard, and we place in Thy hands these who've asked us to pray, and it's written that we should pray one for another. We believe when we pray we're heard by Jesus Christ.

Amen.

Our True Position

Our Father in heaven, we thank Thee for these most revealing, most illuminating, most heartening words of Thy Spirit by the mouth of the servant Paul. We thank Thee for the relationship of the Christian to the Son. We thank Thee that even though all the flesh cries out against it, the truth is that we are joined to Christ and by faith are part of His body, and therefore, the world has only a token claim upon us. But our true position is in the heavenly places in Christ Jesus, where Thou hast blessed us with all spiritual blessing. Help us, we pray, to dare to believe this and to shake off the appeal of earth and of the things of earth, knowing, Lord, that a heart attack or a misjudgment of a second in traffic or something else could soon put an end to all the earth can offer us.

But Thou, O Lord, remainest and we are to be Thine forever. And what we lay up above remains there forever to enjoy, without selfishness, in peace and in holiness before Thee forever. God, help us to see this and live like it. Get hold of our hearts these days, O Lord, we pray Thee, and revive us that we may throw from us the bindings—the tiny, little cords. One of them we can break. Two of them we can break. Ten of them we can break. But when they become so many that they're woven into a great rope, then, Lord, Thou knowest how they bind Thy people. Save and deliver us, we pray Thee, from the bondage of little things.

Keep Thy hand upon us. Lift us up, we pray, and help us to obey Thy Word in all things. Would Thou bless Thy work around the earth? Remember the sick. Remember and restore Thy servants to us. Remember this brother and let Thy will be done in his life. Others that are ill, O God. And help our young people at school and in the service. May mercy attend them, and may they have sweet memories of the home church and prayer and song and worship and the friendly faces they left reluctantly. Keep Thy hand upon us now through the rest of this service. We ask in Jesus' holy name.

Amen.

9

INTERCESSION

PRAYER IS NOT ONLY THE GREATEST force in the universe, but that force is available to the children of God. Prayer makes old people young, and it makes young people wise beyond their years. I would rather trust to the wisdom of a praying man twenty-five years old, than I would to the wisdom of a man seventy-five years old who didn't pray, for I don't think we ought ever to listen to any man that doesn't first listen to God. The praying young man will have greater wisdom than the prayerless old man. But the praying old man will have the happiness or usefulness of the young man. Could it be that a praying man is really a young man inside? You don't know it, but a praying man stays young, and a praying young man gets old in experience and knowledge. I believe so.

Prayer robs adversity of its power and makes poor men rich. It smooths the dying pillow. You know, one of these days you're going to die. Do you know how well you're going to die? You're going to die just as well as you've prayed. No better and no worse. You're smoothing your dying bed now. My God, how awful it must be for those who live carelessly and prayed a little, to try in that last frantic hour to pack into those few precious minutes what should have been a lifetime.

Thankfully, prayer keeps the dead saints alive and keeps them yet speaking. Old Milton wrote about the flowers that were born to blush unseen and waste their fragrance on the desert air. He talked about the jewels at the deep depths of ocean bare. I don't think there's any child of God that ever needs to be a flower that's born unseen to waste its fragrance on the desert air. The praying saint doesn't die. The praying saint lives on in his prayers, and the power of God comes to this place and that place long after a man is gone.

Listen to me, friends: do you think God Almighty is blessing America today because we have a certain administration? Do you think He'll bless her more if we turn out one party and put in the other? No, God isn't blessing America today because of anybody that's in the White House or in the Senate. God is blessing America today because, unseen by mortal eyes but seen plainly by the eyes of God, there are little spirals and incense rising to the right hand of God from the holy graves where lie men and women who once thought and prayed and loved and sacrificed and suffered and died. They prayed and God put their prayers in little bottles, and then they died and were laid away in their dark tombs. And still, their prayers are rising to God. It's the unseen spirals of holy prayer, rising to God like sweet incense from an altar.

Completed Redemption

O Lord, we offer our prayers in the name of Him who was smitten for our salvation. We read our individual names into the record and hide us in the wounds of the Savior, and step under the shadow of His cross and take refuge in His open side. We cry, "Rock of Ages, cleft for me, let me hide myself in Thee. Let the water and the blood from Thy riven side which flowed, be of sin the double cure, save me from its wrath and power."

Lord, we thank Thee that the way into the Presence has been well marked. A wayfaring man, though a fool, may not need to err in it, but it is well marked. The red posts pointing all the same way, red with the holy blood that was more precious than that of bulls and goats or the ashes of a heifer sprinkling. We thank Thee, Lord, that the blood of Thy holy Son is enough. We do not ask for more. We do not pray for an imperfect redemption to be completed. We thank Thee for a completed redemption which needs no improvement.

And Father, this morning we ask for our needy ones in this fellowship. Now, there are many away this morning. We pray for them, O God, that they may all find somewhere to go to church this morning. And then, for the rest of the day they may act like Christians and deport themselves as those who belong to the kingdom of God, not the kingdom of man.

We pray for our sick. Remember the little girl who has been

so very seriously burned. Pray for her healing and restoration to health. We pray for our brother this hour. Bring him back to us again in fullness of strength. We pray for our sister, that the work of restoration may be done there in her body. We pray Thee for others who are ill. God bless them, we pray, this morning. There are united prayers for them. Stand by their bedside and make all their beds in their sickness. And in all their affliction, be Thou afflicted and graciously comfort them in their needs. Be Thou with the grave, needy, bleeding, tired, sick, discouraged world today.

My God, the news out of France and Russia and Germany and Washington and London, it could discourage us and drive us to despair. But Thou hast said, "I have overcome the world, be of good cheer," so we're cheerful. We're hopeful, O Lord, as the Israelites were in the dark night when there was thick darkness over all the land. But nevertheless, in every Jewish house, there was a light, and they sang and rejoiced in the light, the miracle Light.

There is light, O God, in the homes of the redeemed and in the church of the Living God and we are not afraid and we're not worried. We don't know how it all will come out, in detail. We are not sure, but we know one thing, that they will be, when the kingdoms of this world shall be, the Kingdom of our God and of His Christ and He shall reign on the earth and it's in Thy hands. My God, we wish it there. We wouldn't want to take the responsibility, nor be in any wise accountable for the doings of man. We leave it in Thy hand, Lord, where it belongs. Thou art the Sovereign God and Thou wilt bring it out. Thou doest all things well. Graciously help us today that we may deport ourselves both outwardly and inwardly as those who worship Thee. We ask it in Christ's name.

Amen.

Intercession for the Church

O, Thou Son of God, Thou most holy Lamb, we're here as Thy servants this evening. Oh, we thank Thee, Lord, we're not all that there are. We thank Thee, Father, that there are many others. Thank Thee this is not the only church. Thank Thee, Lord, that it isn't a choice between the Alliance church and Hell, for there are thousands of churches on this continent where just as true and wonderful truth is preached, and many of them in this city. For this we thank Thee this night and give Thee praise, Father, Lord of heaven and earth, for all the good churches and good preachers and good, faithful men of God.

But Father, there are churches that fatten and grow on those who won't take the narrow way. Great God, pity and spare this refuge for cowards, these great ornate edifices dedicated to the deserters, paid for by the cowards, kept up by the ignoble deserters from the army of God. Have mercy on such. Oh, have mercy on such.

But bless every gospel church, Lord. Bless every gospel church, whatever denomination. Bless every man that stands to preach tonight. And Father, some of them will stand with robes on, but they'll preach the Word. Some choirs tonight, wearing robes, will sing the wonders of redemption. Blessed be Thy name. Thou lookest not on the outward appearance, but on the heart.

We bless Thee and worship Thee tonight. We have found the way, past the veil, through the blood, to the Holy of Holies with God. Blessed be Thy name.

Now Lord, we pray Thee for any who may be discouraged, who may be having a hard time, who may have been secretly toying with throwing it all up and saying, "what's the use?" They've been tempted, maybe even fallen for the temptations. Great God, have mercy upon Thy sheep tonight, Thy poor bruised, battered sheep. Satan and wolves and bears, they've been after Thy sheep. Their jaws are slavering and their eyes are keen and sharp and penetrating, and their paws are soft as they pad around waiting. O Lord, save Thy sheep tonight. Bless this truth. Show us plainly, through it, that there's nowhere to go. But show us also that Thou art the Christ, the Son of the Living God, that Christ who should come and turn our feet toward Thee as well as our hearts. Help us now as we wait upon Thee, Father, through Jesus Christ our Lord.

Amen.

Taught of God

Father, we heard Thy Son say, "Thine they were and Thou gavest them me" and "I give unto them eternal life; and they shall never perish." And we hear Thy Son say, they shall all be taught of God. And they that hear and are taught of the Father: "They should come to me, and whoever comes to me, I will in no wise cast out."

We pray for these who have requested us to pray. Lord, not I, but Thyself, Thou art inviting these friends. Wilt Thou, we beseech Thee, continue to work deep within their hearts? Satan has every trap baited, every dead fall, every pit. They're all ready to catch unwary sinners. Lord Jesus, Thou didst come to seek and to save that which was lost, and we pray that these might know Thee, Thy saving grace, Thy saving grace, a saving knowledge, we'll never regret it. We'll never regret it. Nobody ever has yet. Nobody ever will, for wisdom is justified.

Keep Thy hand upon us, we pray. May it please Thee that these should believe and move over into and enter into a place of quiet and complete trust. You're the perfect Savior. Grant that it may be so tonight in Jesus' name.

Amen.

Hearts Turned Back

O Lord, Lord, Thou hast brought life and immortality to light through the gospel. Thou hast set a candle in every Christian grave. Thou hast sanctified every floating Christian body in the vast sea. Thou hast sanctified every dried flick of dust that was once the tabernacle of the Holy Ghost. Great God, Thou hast taken the darkness out of the future. Thou hast set a thousand suns there. We thank Thee Thou hast made the bitterest pain tolerable. Thou hast taught us to so number our days as those whose days are given as a school for the world to come.

We pray for any who may be lost in this room tonight. We pray they may turn their hearts back to Thee, back to the Scriptures, back to the cross, back to the blood, back to the Savior.

O God, for our young people! O God, Thou knowest this terrible day. O God, Thou knowest this terrible day! We're inventing vaccines to keep them from dying of polio, and we're keeping them alive to teach them to be fools, and to live like fools, and die like fools. My God, how confused everything is! We're licking one disease after another. We pushed life expectancy up from thirty-four years to sixty-some years. All those years that we've gained on earth, we're wasting.

My God, forgive us. We're stupid. We are as beasts before Thee, O Lord. My God, we pray nobody might go out of this building tonight that hasn't found Thee as his God and Jesus

Thy Son as his Savior, that doesn't know that immortality has come to him in essence, in eternal life and fact. That now he can spread his wings and soar out and rise and become enamored of those things, for Christ sitteth at the right hand of God.

O my Father, don't let anybody here tonight be lost, we pray. Save our young people from the nonsense and foolishness and chatter, and all the devil-inspired traps and tricks that would ruin them. Save them from their own lusts. Save them from their own high spirits and hot blood. Save them from their pool of ignorance. Great God, save our young people. Save them all. Add to their numbers. Make them such magnets that they'll draw other young people in off the street. They would wait for them to grow up from the kindergarten, but they'll come in off the street to see what makes these young people happy-faced.

My Father, do something for us. Spread the gospel message. Bless every man who at this hour, in this city, may be ending his sermon and inviting people to the front. Bless we pray, every gospel preacher. May Satan suffer a major defeat tonight and the kingdom of God a major victory, receive a major victory. Help us now, as we wait upon Thee, in Christ's name.

Amen.

Cleansed of Sin

O Lord Jesus, Thou knowest there's a little fruit. Maybe they're not very big yet, the grapes are not very plentiful, but they're there. And they're a happy assurance that we're branches indeed, joined by life to the Vine. And we hear Thee singing as Thou dost walk around among the branches.

And here, Lord, are probably fifty people or more—sixty, maybe. We stand out of this audience tonight. For the rest, Lord, we're not accusing and we're not reflecting. They know their own minds. And we leave them with Thee. Perhaps they've already, some of them, made this arrangement and settled this covenant. But for those who stand, O God, at this hour, we pray Thee, take each one by the hand and lead them in the way they should go. Save them, we pray Thee, from every vestige, every old, tattered piece of sinful rag that clings to them as it clung to Lazarus when he came out of the grave. Thou didst say, "Unloose him," and they had to unwrap him. Oh, unwrap, we pray Thee, Thy people. Take off all the grave clothes, the mold, and everything that belongs to the sinful life. Cleanse it, purge it, and snip it off, one thing after another. And if they bleed a little and hurt a little, we're sorry, but O God, we wouldn't have it otherwise.

We want to be holy rather than be comfortable. So wilt Thou grant to lead these children forward until they shall become indeed fruit bearers, much fruit for the glory of the Father and to the glory of the Vine, Jesus Christ our Lord? Don't let them forget this. May this be a sacred moment, as they covenant and stand and wait before Thee.

Amen.

Destroy the Enemy

O Christ, Thou hast told us that we were to abide in Thee and then Thou hast told us how we could know we were abiding in Thee: by keeping Thy words and loving as Thou didst love and obey Thine commandments, which are easy, and Thy yoke is light.

Now, Lord, if Satan has got at some, and the flesh and the devil collaborated to hurt Thy sheep to scar and make the branches bleed, we pray Thee tonight, look us over. And, O Lord Jesus, we beseech Thee, wilt Thou grant to perfect that which pertaineth to us? We pray for any who may think they're Christians but are not. Father, for Christ's sake, hear us and strip away false ceilings and get right down at the heart of things. Thy blessing and grace, we beseech Thee, be here this evening, actively engaged by the Spirit and working in human hearts.

Lord, we pray for these men who've said "pray for me." We beseech Thee that Thou wilt destroy their enemy from before them, that Thou will beat down the foes from before their face.

We beseech Thee that Thou, Lord, wilt come in like a flood of water to raise them off the sandbars and to float them, to get them afloat on the sea of Thy grace. We pray that the blessed Holy Ghost within them may wrestle, and work, and thrash about, until He's torn loose their moorings or the chains and has got them out on the sea, where they can be freed under the broad starry heavens above to do the will of the Father.

Lord God, our figures are all mixed up, but our hearts, Thou knowest what they are. My Lord and my God, these people want to be branches on a vine. They want to be friends of the Lord Jesus. They want to be children of the Most High. They want to be sheep of His pasture. They want to be sons of His love. They want to be soldiers in His army. Great God, grant that Thy whole, mighty, living, rich purpose for them might be fulfilled right away.

Now, let Thy grace be upon us all here tonight. We thank Thee, Father, for the good grace that is ours and for these faithful Christians. But we pray they might go on to be hard on themselves, uncharitable toward themselves but loving toward everybody else, severe with themselves but kindly toward everyone else. Be gracious to us, Lord. We ask it in Thy name, the name of Thy Son, Jesus.

Amen.

Forward Commitment

Lord Jesus, Lord Jesus, "In the beginning was the Word, and the Word was with God, and the Word was God. The same was in the beginning with God" (John 1:1–2). We thank Thee, Lord Jesus, that when we come to Thee, we go back to the beginning. We go back of Paul and back of Moses, back of Abraham, back of Adam, we go back to the beginning—the Light that shineth and lighteth every man. In Thee we see the Father; through Thee we know the Father.

We pray for these who've requested prayer tonight. In the name of Thy Son Jesus, we pray, Father, that Thou wilt take these young people and these older ones and lead them in deep pastures and green pastures and through ways that may be rough and hard, and even painful and chastening, but lead them, Lord, lead them, until all is behind them, everything's behind them, and they put behind them everything—everything—what they were, what they are, what they're proud of, what they're ashamed of, what the victories they've had and the defeats they've had and the mistakes they've made.

Oh, we pray Thee, lead these friends on and teach them how to look forward and not backward, and seek Thy Face. We know, Father, that when we talk about these things, some come because they feel that they will be given a capsule which they can swallow, or a text they can memorize, or one little trick they can do. O Lord God, it is not thus received, but rather by the cultivation of the knowledge of God in Christ Jesus, by faith and humility and prayer and trust and confidence and obedience, and by the pressing onward until at last the mountaintop appears in view, and out of the mist we come to the sunlight.

Come, Holy Spirit, heavenly dove. Come with all Thy quickening power. Come, we pray Thee, and shed abroad the Savior's love that it may quicken ours. We pray for all of these. Then we pray, Lord, for some who didn't request prayer for anything, but who should have and who perhaps are this night without even salvation.

And we pray for all the churches that are bringing their service to close right now or will be within a half an hour. So bless them all, Lord, and grant, we pray Thee, that every net may have fishes, that every shepherd may find lost sheep and every father sees sons come home, and that there be victory in the church of Jesus Christ this night, we pray Thee. To Thee we give praise. We ask this thing through Jesus Christ our Lord.

Amen.

Vessels unto Honor

O Jesus Christ, we pray Thee for these young people who've stood. We pray Thee for these boys, these young men, and these young women. O God, we pray that Thou wilt polish the lenses of their soul that the light might shine through. We pray that Thou wilt help them to hate lust and hate filth and hate iniquity. Help them, we pray Thee, like Jesus Thy Son; as He was, let them be. "Thou hast loved righteousness, and hated iniquity; therefore God, even thy God, hath anointed thee" (Heb. 1:9).

Oh, we pray Thee, turn these friends around to love that which is holy and hate that which is bad, and to be meek and humble and lowly and tractable and teachable. Let them be soft clay in Thy hand to be made into vessels unto Thy honor. Grant this for Christ's sake.

Amen.

Led by God

O Lord Jesus, we sang about Thee tonight and our hearts sang. We were telling Thee who Thou art, the mighty Lord, King of kings, God made flesh to dwell among us. O Lord Jesus, our Joshua, lead us. Thou hast brought us out of Egypt's bondage. We've been born of the Spirit and we're now the children of the Father. But, O Christ, Thou knowest what poor examples of Christians some of us have been: temper, grouchiness, jealousy, lust, carnal ambition, inordinate affection, fear—all these things are hinted, and they are the Amorites and the Hittites and the Jebusites.

Thou hast said, "I will lead thee in on to the land of thine enemies." And every one of these enemies is a friend turned wrong side up, and every place where these enemies are camped or have their cities, they're ours by right of blood. And Lord, wilt Thou lead the people in, Lord, lead them in? We thank Thee. It isn't long until everybody knows that something wonderful has happened to that Christian. But mostly we drag our feet.

O Lord, grant that these who've raised their hands tonight and asked us to pray may cease to be at ease in Zion, push their way on by obedience and faith into a place opened for us by Jesus Christ. We thank Thee, Lord. There's nothing but what has been purchased for us on the cross. We thank Thee when Thou didst die there, and when the spear let out the water and the blood, that we can say as the poet said, "Let the water and the blood from Thy riven side which flowed, be of sin the double cure." Lord, this double cure—people don't believe much in it, but there's a double cure. We pray Thee, help us that we may know the double cure by the blood.

Bless these friends, every one of them. We ask Thee to disturb them. Upset them. Don't let them find rest until they find it in Thee. Their heart's too big to find rest in things. Thou hast made their hearts too vast to find rest in trifle. It would be as ridiculous as a married couple getting married and settling for a parakeet. Lord God, Thou hast given us hearts big enough to take in a family, not a parakeet, Lord. Thou hast given the

Christians hearts big enough to take in all the land of promise, and we settle for a little barren patch in the wilderness. God forgive us, and let the Spirit of God guide over the next few days these friends. Let them push forward and enter. Lead us, oh, lead us, blessed Jesus. We thank Thee Thou wilt.

Amen.

Darkness to Light

O blessed Jesus, blessed Lord Jesus, Thou didst come to a world of sin and death and darkness. Thou didst come with holiness and life and light. And Thou didst call unto Thee all who would come and say, "Come unto me ... and I will give you rest" (Matt. 11:28).

Now, we beseech Thee, Lord, that Thou wilt help us. Most of us here tonight are Christians, if not all. We pray that we may be saved from ourselves, saved from the downward tug of the world and from the gravitational pull of the flesh, from the stirrings of the old man and from the pressures of sloganeers and advertisers and smooth religionists and oozing politicians. Help us to stay free and clean and separated from it all, looking and expecting until that hour when Thou shalt come for Thy people.

Great God, we pray for the poor world. We pray for those who will be caught in the snare. We pray for all those who dwell on the earth who are the innocent victims, in some measure, of their evil leadership, political leadership, educational leadership, religious leadership. It is preparing people to become victims, to follow like poor sheep the evil shepherd. Keep Thou, we pray Thee, Thy hand upon us and let Thy grace attend us.

Now, may grace and mercy and peace be upon us through Jesus Christ our Lord, and all God's children said amen.

Outward Prayers

We're here this evening in this house dedicated to the hearing of the Truth and the worship of the Trinity. And we're gathered here, Lord, out of the world. And there are many other groups like this gathered all over the world. Some larger, some smaller, and even the vast assemblies and little handfuls, but added together, we thank Thee that we are not a small number, but a great number.

And add to those the ones that are with Thee and it's a number no man can count. Innumerable beyond all possibility of numbering. Only Thou, with infinite knowledge, know how many have believed on Thy Son and have been washed in the blood of the Lamb and are with Thee now. We thank Thee for every one of them, Lord. We wouldn't overlook any. And we thank Thee for those we might not know who are Christians, or that we might in our haste be disqualified. But the Spirit knows who they are and we pray for them tonight, O Lord, all over the earth.

Help behind the iron curtains. Help behind bamboo curtains. Help, Lord, where it's a felony to be a Christian. Help where it's a crime to pray and to believe in Thee. Help, we pray Thee, where the name of the virgin and the name of the saints is more familiar than the name of Jesus Christ the Lord. Help in those lands, O God. Turn things, we pray Thee, around, then graciously bless and grant the time soon when the free gospel may go forth and men shall believe and be transformed because they believe.

Help now, we pray Thee, our God. Help our sick. Help the bereaved and help the troubled and help the distressed. And Lord, we pray that we may not spend all our time on ourselves, but that we may go out, and we may think out, and pray out, and serve out, and send out, until we are a blessing in the world. Until we are like the fragrant rose that grows in the valley, but spreads its fragrance all up and down the valley. Make this company, we pray Thee, to be felt and its fragrance to travel way all over the earth, O God.

Let Thy blessing be upon us this night. Remember our sister and touch that troubled heart of hers. And bless the families with loved ones gone. Oh, we pray, Father, that help may come and blessing may flow and that we may get ourselves adjusted to these things and know, Lord, that in Thy hand there is no death. In Thy heaven, there is no grief and no pain, but all things are right in our Father's house. And Lord, now we thank

Thee that our brother's gone to our Father's house and that he's there, and he's there to join a lot of the others with whom he served here in years gone by. God bless the family, and for him, accept our thanks.

Be with us now as we wait upon Thee, Father, through Jesus Christ our Lord.

Amen.

Kindled Truth

Now, our Father, we well know that spiritual things can't be reduced to formulas, even though we struggle so hard to do it. An impulsive faith and a sudden reckless daring of the soul would do more for us than all the carefully laid out sermons could ever do. But we've done all we can do. We appeal to the intelligence, made some explanations, tried to say in our modern English what has been said with great and stately dignity in our Bibles.

My God, now take this that's been spoken and apply it to our hearts. May we, one after the other, turn from Adam's unbelieving world with its self-confidence, its self-reliance, its arrogance, its pride, its mad pleasures, its love of wealth, love of praise, its love of publicity, its inordinate love of clothing and of fine things and of rich things. Turn us, we pray Thee, from it all, not only in our hearts but in reality. And then turn us to

Jesus Christ Thy Son. We need Him, Lord. If we gave up the world and didn't have Him, we'd be in a vacuum. Would Thou quickly take us to Thy little vacuum and take us to Jesus Christ who is the radiant source of everlasting life and peace and joy, world without end.

Would Thou bless us now as we go on into the Lord's Supper? We ask it in Christ's name.

Amen.

10

SPIRITUAL LIVING

WHAT DOES PRAYER MEAN TO YOU? I believe it's only a religious cliché to repeat that prayer is the greatest privilege ever granted to men. That the Ancient of Days, high and lifted up, should so stoop down and condescend to listen to the prayers of such ones as you and I who are sinners by nature and for a while by choice. Little men and women with breath in our nostrils, with our tiny hearts beating away, ready to stop one of these days and let us collapse, hopeless chunks of clay and animated dust that we are.

That the great God Almighty who made the sun and flung it against the darkness, and who made the stars and studded the skies with them, and who cut out the rivers and pushed up the mountains and girded the world. He made man upon it and gave him food and the air to breathe and water to drink. That this great God should bend His ear like a mother bending over a sick child, trying to catch the faintest whisper meant to catch the ear of love. That, I say, is the greatest privilege in all the world. Therefore, prayer should be the most sacred thing in the world and it should be made with the greatest sense of thanksgiving and gratitude.

Not only is prayer the highest honor that can be granted to any being, it's the most profitable investment in all the world. For example, I've had this experience and I suppose some of you have as well, of having the weight of the whole world on your back. Talk about Atlas carrying the world on his shoulder. And you too have felt this weight of all things, and you've dropped to your knees with your open Bible and have gotten still and quiet, read the Word, looked up to God and not asking for much, but looked up to God and got calm and got orientated and adjusted to God in your own soul. And pretty soon the world began to roll off of Atlas' back and the burden began to roll off your shoulders and you stood up rested and felt as good as if you had been three weeks in Florida.

I have been on the brink when if I had just gone five minutes longer, I would have resigned the church and quit the ministry, and maybe run off from home. But by the grace of God, there's such a thing as making a profitable investment in prayer just for what it'll do for you inside. The tuning up of your instrument as for the harmonizing of the soul within you. And yet, while it is certainly the greatest, most profitable thing, it is also the hardest thing in the world for Christians to do. Prayer is the hardest thing in all the world, and you know why? Because you have to be right with God to pray.

Help and Hope

O God our Father, God our Father, this night, the world has grown old and the judgment draws near. Kingdoms have risen and waned. Nation has risen against nation and kingdom against kingdom. As it was in the days of Noah, so is it now, in this day. These are solemn times. We appeal to Thee, O Lord, we appeal to Thee. Help us in this hour. Help us now.

We beseech Thee, O Lord, for the cringing sinner, for the frightened, cowering sinner who hasn't the courage to get up and follow the Lamb, but who's trying to get in somehow, through some window or back door. God, have mercy, we pray Thee, this hour through Jesus Christ. Help us in this moment of decision. We ask it in Jesus' name.

Amen.

Cultivated Life

Dear Lord, Thou art in this place, and we know it not. We find this, the gate of heaven and the very house of God, and we enter as though it were the sidewalk or the back lot. Cleanse us, O Lord, from our blindness and help us to see Thee as Thou art: Lord of lords, King of kings and Majesty unspeakable in breadth. Thou art here. Let all the earth be silent before Thee. We pray that Thou wilt speak to us out of the Holy Word. Speak Lord, Thou hast gifted men. Thou hast given gifts unto men, and Thou hast sent those men to speak to the churches.

We pray that tonight we may hear through the gifts of the Spirit the unspeakable riches of Christ and the wondrous words of prophecy. We pray that Thou this evening will give us ears that can hear and hearts that can understand. Give us wills, quick to obey. Give us faith, that we may believe. Save us, we pray Thee, from the sheer numbers that the world has and from the psychology of numbers, and from all the lies out there that surround us. Save us from it, O Lord, and give us Christian hearts and help us to think as Christians think. We have the mind of Christ. Great God, help us, that we might, this night, exercise the mind of Christ as we think over spiritual things.

Wilt Thou bless this great city, the city, Lord, that can be made to go wild over practically nothing at all? And when it's all over and added up, it didn't amount to anything, and yet, day follows day when men will pack their cars miles, bumper to bumper and stand, like grass on the lawn, like a carpet of human beings covering acres to see what finally turns out to be nothing. O Lord, we pray Thee, lift our eyes to behold those wonders that, alas, those mysteries that will never fade away. Those amazing sights that make the angels to wonder and rejoice.

And grant, we pray Thee, that this evening we may yet behold Thy face and we may get help in our hearts, help in our lives and in our inner beings, we may get help. The world lies out there, Father, and we've got to face it tomorrow and the next day and the next, and on until Thou dost call us home. Lord, we pray Thee that we may as Jacob, by the brook Jabbok, met Thee and then went out to face his brother, his angry brother, the next day on the plain.

We pray, help us this night, by this brook, that we may be so refreshed and so blessed that when we go up tomorrow to face an angry, hostile world, that we'll go with all the success Jacob had. And that our names might be Israel, Thou hast prevailed. Give us, we pray, prevailing faith. We have it, Lord, we will have it, we do have it. We have faith in the Christ who is conqueror, who is victorious, who has risen from the dead, who is seated in power and majesty, and all things belong to Him. Now, we're trusting Thee, believe Thou hast heard us, and we shall tonight be greatly helped in this service. In Christ's name.

Amen.

Cleansed Inner Man

We pray Thee, Lord Jesus, to bless these friends. Time is rolling on, unceasingly, never stops. The power is never turned off. Never is there a turning backward. Never is there the reliving of one day twice, no one hour twice. We're moving on, Lord. Nature and time are beating us out. Our bodies are soon to perish like the grass and be cut off.

But our inner man, our inner man, our "I," is waiting there.

O Lord, we pray we may take care of our inner man. We pray that which we variously call our spirit, our soul, our inner man, may come to know of the cleansing, the purifying water. We may be clean and right and good and ready for life or death.

Bless these who've listened this morning. Turn their thoughts toward Thee. Make us spiritual people who worship God in spirit and in truth. Save us, Father, from outward things. Save us from the inartistic, bizarre, crass spirit of Christmas. We see all around about us great glaring chunks of green and red, and coarse out-of-focus horns bellowing out "Silent Night." All this is exceedingly offensive to the child of God who has an inner life. We pray Thee, save us from getting caught in the world, and feed our inner life for Jesus' sake.

Amen.

Fresh Delivery

O God, we thank Thee for Thy most noble words. These comforting, wholesome, heavenly words that fall like manna out of heaven. And we are tempted to stand back with reverence and say, what is this? We know not what it is and cry, manna! These are mysterious words. Truth, words from Thee to feed us and to nourish us, even here in our earthly pilgrimage.

Now, we pray Thy blessing to rest upon us in this morning worship hour. Father, we pray, make it as new as Thou dost make the morning. No morning is monotonous, though it's like the one before it and like the one that will follow it. It is fresh. We pray Thee, make Thy mercies fresh. Make our songs and all that we do and think to be as fresh as the new dew-washed morning that comes with the rising of the sun. Give us fresh hearts, hearts as childlike as it is necessary they should be, in order that we may not offend Thee by pride or sophistication or a perfunctory spirit as we go through our worship.

Give us, O Lord we pray, hearts that can worship Thee indeed, acceptable in Thy sight through Jesus Christ our Lord. We pray for the work which Thou hast given us to do, each doing his part over this whole earth. Bless every man who honors Thee and whose intention is to help mankind and promote the high honor of the Most High God. Whether that man speaks our language quietly, or goes with our company. No one can do service for Thee and speak lightly of Thee. O Lord, we pray that such may be helped today, and Thy blessing may rest upon all of Thy work throughout all the earth. Raise up the fallen. Help the discouraged. Heal the sick, and give faith to expect the answers to all that we ask. In the name of Jesus Christ, our Lord.

Amen.

Honored Service

Father, we thank Thee for Thyself. We thank Thee for Thy character. We thank Thee for Thy being. One God, one Majesty. There is no God but Thee, unextended, uncreated Unity. O God, we bless Thee.

Now we pray Thee, send these Christians out to be not hothouse plants but soldiers. Take advantage of the promises to fill their minds and carry them back to the God that made them, to use them as weapons, tools in the warfare. O God, Satan has laughed at our futile prayers. Help us now to go out and make him laugh on the other side of his face. He's been too long in possession of the fields.

O God, for this church, for this church—we claim victory for this church. Him that honors Thee wilt Thou honor, and O God, we want to honor Thee. We want to honor Thee by telling truth. We want to honor Thee by being fair. We want to honor Thee by telling all sides of every question and not cheating, not lying, and not using advertising techniques to succeed, but to tell the old, old story that men have loved so well. Continue to tell it, and honestly. We honor Thee, O God, and look to Thee to honor us and our ministry and our church and our people and our praying.

We ask Thee tonight, our God, as we close this meeting, for another new surge, another new lurch forward. A few months ago we heard You say, "Consider no more the old things; lo,

I will do a new thing." Thou hast done it for us. Thou hast brought up our Sunday school. Thou hast enlarged us. Thou hast let us have branches over the wall. Thou hast helped us. And now Lord, we're encouraged to believe Thee at what You promise You'll do. And we pray Thee for another lurch, O God. We've taken some ground. Now we're going to take some more ground.

Together we're united to prayer, to fellowship in our homes, everywhere. And all the brethren and sisters and young people, children that make up our fellowship, shall see a Fall and Winter that will confuse the devil and confound his purposes and cause all the people to say, "O God, we give you praise." We count on this, our Father and Jesus Christ our Lord. And this is the confidence that we have in Thee, that if we ask anything according to Thy will, Thou dost hear us, and if Thou dost hear us, whatsoever we ask, we have the petitions that we've asked of Thee. Unitedly, we take these petitions for a larger missionary offering, a larger outreach of spiritual fellowship, and larger influence in the whole evangelical church, that we might come back again to simplicity, honesty, modesty, meekness, scripture, worship, holiness and the power of the Spirit of God. Grant it for Jesus' sake, we pray.

Amen.

Forward Movement

Now Father, wilt Thou bless all who listened tonight? Wilt Thou grant, we pray, that we may forget the things that are behind and press forward toward the things that are ahead? And that we may see all that is as being only the size of a hazelnut, and see that God is vast—so vast—that we encompass the world and are utterly empty without Thee! Fill us, O God, fill us with Thyself, for without Thee, we will be ever wanting. Fill us with Thyself, for Jesus Christ's sake.

Amen.

Always Ready

O dear Lord, when we stand outside of ourselves and think as the world thinks, how foolish is a talk like this tonight. How different from politics and philosophy and psychology and sports and entertainment and labor and capital and industry and all the rest. Thou hast called us, O Lord, and enlightened us, called us to Thyself and given us information, and our language sounds strange and remote and unlike the world. Nothing like this is found in newspapers or magazines for the world doesn't know a thing about it. The world is going on its way, doing the best it can.

Oh, Thou hast called a people for Thine own possession, a royal priesthood, a holy nation, a peculiar people, a cross-carrying people who love Thy holy Son and call Thee Father, who believe the prophets and the apostles, who believe the book of Revelation, who believe what John saw in the Spirit. Oh, that we might be among them!

Oh, that we might be counted in that blessed group. That it not only be ready in that day, but ready now, and we'll be ready and continue to be ready and will labor to get others ready, and struggling and fight and pray and give and push and carry on the work until the story has been told around the world and the globe is girdled with the gospel—at least one time—so that red and yellow and black and white around this whole world can know that Christ died for our sins according to the Scriptures and that He rose again, according to the Scriptures. Help us now, Father, we pray.

Now, we're going out into a week that promises to be hot and it's going to be busy, noisy, and there will be irritations, hostility and trouble, weakness, physical discomforts and pains. Oh, enable us to rejoice in it all, to be glad and thank Thee and to keep full of praise and to meet every trouble with praise. Help us to keep praised up and prayed up. Help us to put behind us everything that would hinder us and lay aside every weight and the sin that does so easily beset us, and run with patience the race set before us. This we ask through Jesus Christ our Lord.

Amen.

Putting Adam Behind

Our Father, we are refreshed in mind and heart as we read again the true record and hear the words of the Spirit telling us that He ascended up on high. We thank Thee for Christ Jesus, the Lord, our Savior. And we pray that Thou wilt help us now that we may put away Adam's way of looking at things. We've been with Adam this week. We've been in the world. We've been in offices and shops and stores and everywhere where Adam is.

Now, Lord Jesus, Thou second Adam, we pray Thou help us that we may purge out of our thinking Adam's ways of thinking and Adam's psychology, and that we may think as Christians. Think, as if this morning Christ had risen today, that this was the morning that He rose from the dead and that He is now among us alive, eternally alive, and death hath no more dominion over Him. We pray that Thou would grant that around this living, risen, glorified man was also God.

We may gather today. We may gather in our thoughts. We gather in our hearts and in all that we may feel and know that the Lord is with us, and that we're not alone. That we're not trying to promote a service or manufacture one, but that we, as the disciples of old, simply gather around our risen Lord.

Would Thou remember the poor and the helpless today, and the sick and the distressed? And help among the nations of the world, O God. Thou knowest we see fulfilled before us the strange, dramatic pictures which Daniel wrote and painted for us. And we see and hear the words of our Lord being fulfilled when He told us of wars and commotions and rumors of wars and the hearts of men failing them for fear of things that are taking place on the earth. Oh, we pray that instead of our being depressed by all this, we may rejoice because our redemption draws nigh.

Wilt Thou help us all over the earth? Wilt Thou remember Thy work so badly hindered by the devil in so many places? We pray Thee, O God, Thou wouldst help in Laos today. Help, we pray Thee, in Vietnam. Help, we pray, in Indonesia, and in other parts where the conditions, political conditions, make it dangerous and sometimes impossible for Thy people to work. They have almost marked time waiting for Thee to open the door.

We ask that Thou wilt bless those out from this church on the many fields of the world and in many pulpits throughout the world and sitting at many organ consoles and standing to lead choirs and teaching in schools. O God, bless Thou, we pray, that stream of blessed humanity that's gone out from this small church to all parts of the world over the last years. Help us to pray for them and keep praying for them.

Now Lord, bless us as we wait further upon Thee. We ask this through Jesus Christ our Lord.

Amen.

Loving Anticipation

Our Father in heaven, we are before Thee, both with encouragement and fear. For we fear Thee, O Thou living God, Almighty as Thou art. But we're cheered by the memory that Thou has stooped to ask of us the love of our poor heart. And so we walk the happy and awesome path between open fear. We hope in the Lord. We hope in the blood. We hope in the cross. And we thank Thee that our hope has underneath it all a solid foundation of inspired truth.

Now also we come reverently, though boldly, unto the throne of grace to receive mercy and grace to help us in our time of need. Father, Thou seest this city that has been so long stricken with bad weather and changing social conditions until the churches have been ground, many of them, as this one has. But Lord, we thank Thee that we're learning from tribulation to be patient and to wait on Thee with the knowledge that, if Thou dost not answer on Sunday, Thou will answer on Monday and if not on Monday, then on Wednesday; if not in February, then in March, for Thou art not excited nor anxious, and Thou dost not rush to do things. Thou dost do them with the calm of eternity.

We bless Thee. Teach us also, we pray Thee, to be calm as those who've been called out of time to live in eternity. At the graveside we say "called out of time into eternity," but we remember this morning that we now—living—are called out of time. And that we live in the Eternal Heart that knows no aging, knows no sunrise or sunset, no yesterday nor tomorrow, one eternal, eternal now. Help us to live then, we pray Thee, with an all-ready, the calm of the age-less eternity in our hearts.

Wilt Thou remember our country? Remember this land, so favored and so, so sinning. Our princes and our leaders and our fathers and our statesmen, our politicians, our preachers, our people—we have sinned against Thee, O Lord, and we have no excuse to offer and no extenuating circumstances to plead. We have sinned. And we deserve, O Lord, only that Thou shouldst deal with us in severe judgment. But Thou art a God of infinite kindness and great goodness and mercy to infinitude. So wilt Thou be merciful unto our land? Be merciful unto our homes. Be merciful, we pray, unto our forty-nine states. Be merciful unto our churches.

Have pity today, O God, upon us all, this first day of this first Sunday of the month when many churches, a great many churches, will be having their Communion service. Lord, we're disappointed in these Communion services. So often we're disappointed—it's so mechanical. We pray, help, that as we drink today of the fruit of the grape, we'll remember that it is the blood of Jesus Christ, shed for us. And as we eat of the bread broken, we'll remember that it is the body of Jesus, that Thou art here in some mysterious and mystic way, present in the now. We believe in the real presence, and so, if the real presence is in the Communion, it's everywhere else too.

So, let us not say a careless word nor think a careless thought, but to live this hour we will be together here, no better, no worse than we lived this morning or we live this afternoon. May every hour be a holy hour and every day a holy day and every place, holy ground. We wait on Thee with expectation through Jesus Christ our Lord.

Amen.

SOURCES

Sermons preached 1953–1959 at Southside Alliance Church, Chicago, and transcribed from original tape recordings.

CHAPTER ONE—JESUS CHRIST

Chapter Introduction: "Conditions for Answers to Prayer," March 11, 1956.

The Good Shepherd: "The True Shepherd vs. the Hireling," March 20, 1955.

Complete in Him: "The Voice of the Holy Spirit," June 14, 1953.

The God-Man: "The Unpopularity of Jesus and His Doctrine," October 31, 1954.

Led by Him: "He That Is Of The Earth Is Earthy, He That Is from Above Is Above All," March 28, 1954.

Adopted: "Doors of Hope," September 19, 1954.

Altar of Sacrifice: "Attitudes and Relationships," March 25, 1956.

Cleansed by the Lamb: "The Marriage Supper of the Lamb," July 26, 1959.

CHAPTER THREE—WORD OF GOD

Chapter Introduction: "Prayer For the Glory of God" No. 1, November 17, 1957.

Plainly Speaking: "The Voice of Reason," June 21, 1953.

Gracious Promises: "The Defiled World and Our Undefiled Inheritance," August 16, 1953.

The Eternal Word: "After Conversion, the Remainder of Our Lives Is to Be Different," June 6, 1954.

Truthful Words: "It Is Possible to Know Whether We Love Christ," December 11, 1955.

Illuminated Word: "Living in His Righteousness," March 31, 1957.

The Word Fulfilled: Given prior to Paris Reidhead's sermon, November 23, 1958.

Words That Shine: Southside Alliance Missionary Conference, April 12, 1959.

Ancient but True: "Is Anything Too Hard for the Lord?", November 9, 1958.

The Living Word: "Landmarks in the Way," August 2, 1959.

Quick, Powerful, and Sharp: "The Word of God Is Quick, Powerful and Sharp," July 26, 1959.

Hope-Filled Words: "Summary of Year and Exhortations," December 28, 1959.

CHAPTER FOUR—AUTHENTICITY

Chapter Introduction: "Prepare by Prayer," September 22, 1957.

Clean Dwellings: "The Gifts of the Spirit" No. 4, November 4, 1956.

First Century Church: "The Glory of That Which Cannot Be Seen with the Mortal Eye," October 13, 1957.

An Accurate Name: "Zacharias and the Angel Gabriel, a Man of God," August 19, 1956.

Power, Fellowship, and Conformity: "Discovering the Loveliness of Jesus Christ," February 3, 1957.

True Belief: "The Doctrine of the Remnant" No. 1, December 8, 1957.

Something Fresh: "Christianity Is a Divine Thing," January 19, 1958.

New Glory: "These Things Revealed unto Babes," August 31, 1958.

Satisfied Christians: "The Great Multitude before the Throne," May 3, 1959.

Precious Treasure: "A. W. Tozer's Farewell Message to Church," November 8, 1959.

Power and Authority: "A. W. Tozer's Evening Farewell to Church," November 8, 1959.

CHAPTER FIVE—BACKSLIDING

Chapter Introduction: "Believing Prayer," August 21, 1955.

Delivery from Indifference: "Jesus at Supper with Mary and Martha," May 8, 1955.

Understand and See: "Nicodemus—The Need for Utter Sincerity before God," January 31, 1954.

Worldly Dangers: "The Beauteous World as Made by Him," November 1, 1953.

Hear, Understand, and Obey: "How to Grow in Grace," April 28, 1957.

Forgive and Cleanse: "He Came unto His Own and His Own Received Him Not," November 8, 1953.

Dissatisfied Deliverance: "Christ Offers Us Spiritual Power," September 29, 1959.

Cooling Hearts: "Causes of Backsliding," November 28, 1954.

Return to First Love: "Backsliding," September 22, 1957.

Sight Restoration: "The Perfection of God," December 7, 1958.

CHAPTER SIX—SURRENDER

Chapter Introduction: "Worship—God's Great Purpose in Redemption," September 29, 1957.

Yielded Hearts: "On God's Sheep and Their Needs," July 11, 1954.

Love Without Control: "The Benefits of Loving our Lord Jesus Christ," December 18, 1955.

Christian Success: "Three Classes of Man," January 29, 1956.

A Clean Start: "The Enabling Power of the Holy Spirit in Our Lives," April 1, 1956.

Walk Worthy: "Considering Perfection in the Christian Life," January 13, 1957.

Crossing Over: "The Special Christian," January 27, 1957.

CHAPTER SEVEN—PENITENTIAL

CHAPTER EIGHT—THANKFULNESS

Chapter Introduction: "God's Goodness," September 28, 1958.

Protected by Providence: "The Word Became Flesh—The Mystery of It," December 20, 1953.

Greatest Discovery: "The Lord of the Woman at the Well," April 4, 1954.

Grateful and Satisfied: "The Once Born and the Twice Born," February 7, 1954.

Mission Possible: "The Personal Application of Christ's Coming into the World," February 28, 1954.

Bonded in Fellowship: "The Christian's Strange and Fiery Trials," June 27, 1954.

Delightful Discovery: "A Definition of Worship," October 20, 1957.

A Mighty Purgation: "The Law of Moral Gravitation," November 25, 1956.

Heavenly Hearing: "Take Heed How Ye Hear," June 16, 1957.

Grateful for Light: "The Doctrine of the Remnant," December 1, 1957.

Journey to Eternity: "The Manifestation of God's Wisdom," February 2, 1958.

Our True Position: "Hezekiah, Sennacherib, and God," January 11, 1959.

CHAPTER NINE—INTERCESSION

Chapter Introduction: "The Blessing That Lies in Prayer," February 26, 1956.

Completed Redemption: "What Jesus Endured for Our Sake," September 5, 1954.

Intercession for the Church: "From that Time, Many of His Disciples Went Back," October 24, 1954.

Taught of God: "God's Wisdom Is Absolute and Qualified," March 30, 1958.

Hearts Turned Back: "Life after Death—the Death of Lazarus," May 1, 1955.

Cleansed of Sin: "The Vine and the Branches" No. 3, January 29, 1956.

Destroy the Enemy: "The Vine and the Branches" No. 5, February 12, 1956.

Forward Commitment: "That We May Know Him," March 17, 1957.

Vessels unto Honor: "The Fear of God Is Wisdom," January 26, 1958.

Led by God: "Entering the Promised Land," July 13, 1958.

Darkness to Light: "The Beast and the Dragon," July 5, 1959.

Outward Prayers: "The Benefits of Prophecy," January 18, 1959.

Kindled Truth: "The Deeper Spiritual Life," February 5, 1956.

CHAPTER TEN—SPIRITUAL LIVING

Chapter Introduction: "The Blessing That Lies in Prayer," February 26, 1956.

Help and Hope: "The Voice of the Holy Spirit," June 14, 1953.

Cultivated Life: "The Beast and the Dragon," July 5, 1959.

Cleansed Inner Man: "The Peaceful Waters of Shiloh," December 18, 1955.

Fresh Delivery: "As Strangers and Pilgrims, Abstain from Fleshly Lusts," February 21, 1954.

Honored Service: "Believing Prayer," August 21, 1955.

Forward Movement: "God's Immanence and Immensity," September 21, 1958.

Always Ready: "The Church, Satan, and the Antichrist," June 21, 1959.

Putting Adam Behind: "Seven Words—He Is Risen, He Was Taken Up," September 27, 1959.

Loving Anticipation: "Serving Members Make a Serving Church," February 1, 1959.

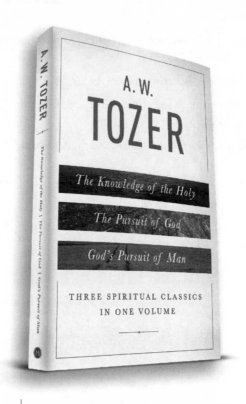